CASEBOOK

FOR

YOUTH MINISTRY

WILLIAM R. CROMER

BROADMAN PRESS
NASHVILLE, TENNESSEE

© Copyright 1991 ● Broadman Press

All Rights Reserved

4260-43

ISBN: 0-8054-6043-8

Dewey Decimal Classification: 259.23

Subject Heading: YOUTH MINISTRY // CHURCH WORK WITH YOUTH

Library of Congress Catalog Number: 90-20445

Printed in the United States of America

Unless otherwise noted, all Scripture quotations are taken from the *King James Version* of the Bible.

All Scripture quotations marked (RSV) are from the *Revised Standard Version of the Bible*, copyrighted 1946, 1952, © 1971, 1973.

Library of Congress Cataloging-in-Publication Data

Cromer, William R., 1923-
    Casebook for youth ministry / William R. Cromer.
        p.   cm.
    ISBN 0-8054-6043-8
    1. Church work with youth. 2. church work with youth—Case
studies.   I. Title.
BV4447.C76   1991
259'.23—dc20   90-20445
                                                                              CIP

To Lois and our sons, Bill, Dan, and Brian,
whose adolescence taught us much
and lives continue to give us
cause for gladness and pride

Contents

Introduction   7
Part 1: Youth and Case Studies.   9
Part 2: Case Studies 17
  1. Ron Scanlon, Teenager. 19
  2. A Trip to Six Flags 32
  3. Youth Camp. 43
  4. Tragedy on a Retreat. 54
  5. Janet Trammel. 66
  6. Freedom to Grow 77
  7. Westport Grass 85
  8. The Prayer Club. 92
  9. Rose Okoni. 102
10. The Bake Sale. 116
11. Lockin 127
12. Lisa's Disappearance. 137
Part 3: Choosing and Using Case Studies. 145
Notes 155

Introduction

The case studies in this book reflect some of the problems faced by "real-life" youth in contemporary American society. In addition, a cross-cultural dimension is added through a case which presents experiences of youth in Nigeria. While no claim is made that all the important problems faced by youth are included in these twelve cases, they do reflect many common ones. In keeping with accepted professional practice, personal identities, places, organizations, and groups are assigned fictitious names to maintain privacy and confidentiality.

Each is designed for study and discussion by a group—youth, leaders, parents, youth ministers, and so forth—under guidance of a well-prepared leader. Group members are expected to become acquainted with the case being used in the group discussion by reading, listening to a tape recording, hearing a monologue, observing a role-play, or other appropriate method of presenting its contents.

The purpose of this book is to provide a helpful vehicle for focusing group study on certain concerns and needs of youth. Those who minister to youth will find the cases interesting and will also discover help in how to write and use them for learning and reflection. Case teaching methodology itself will also be a valuable addition to anyone's skills. A long-range purpose is to encourage readers to research and write cases from their own experiences and use them in all areas of their ministry.

The volume is divided into three sections. Part 1 introduces youth ministry as the genre for the cases and briefly treats their use in the Bible and value for youth ministry. Part 2 presents twelve cases involving youth. Background data and ideas given for each case in "Ponderings for Pedagogy" are unusual, or perhaps even unique, information. Extensive and specific suggestions are then given in "Group Leadership," including supplementary resources.

Part 3 is a resource for case discussion leaders. Concrete suggestions are proposed for selection and use with cases, and techniques for evaluating group discussion of a case are included, along with a specific technique developed and used by the author.

A special effort has been made to provide a variety of group procedures. Ranging from a crossword puzzle, true-false statements, to role-playing, these procedures will help teachers with little or great experience. It is intended that these procedures will stimulate the leader's own "creative juices" and help him or her design uniquely personal pedagogies.

Three of my mentors in case methodology granted permission to use their previously published cases. Robert and Alice Evans, codirectors of the Association of Case Teachers, Simsbury, Connecticut, approved my use of "Freedom to Grow." Louis Weeks, academic dean at Louisville Presbyterian Theological Seminary, Louisville, Kentucky, granted use of his case "Westport Grass."

I acknowledge my indebtedness to the several hundred students who joined me over the past fifteen years in learning more about how to minister to youth through my course entitled "Case Studies in Youth Ministry." Special appreciation is due Michael Adams, Karla Buhl, Philip Hedgecoth, Skip Stephan, Stanley Sonte, and Henry Tyson who have given permission for their cases to be edited and used.

Bill Moxley, my Graduate Fellow in Christian Education, provided valuable research assistance and editorial ideas. His help was made possible by a generous grant from the Eli Lilly Foundation through the administration of Willis Bennett, provost of The Southern Baptist Theological Seminary, Louisville, Kentucky. The critique and helpful suggestions for improvement of the manuscript by my longtime friend and colleague, Ronald Deering, librarian for The Southern Baptist Theological Seminary was also made possible by this grant.

WILLIAM R. CROMER, JR.
Louisville, Kentucky

Part 1
Youth and Case Studies

Youth: They don't understand the real world, the one I live in. I'm under so much pressure. Sometimes I wonder if my parents really care.

Parent: Why can't I seem to understand my kids? A lot of times it is so difficult to know how to help them. They seem to have so many demands and pressures. I know it is not like it was when I was growing up. Sometimes I am really afraid for them.

Lay Leader: I care deeply for these kids. I want to be a friend in whom they can trust and confide when necessary. My hope is that I can reinforce their feelings of self-worth and confidence for coping with their lives.

Youth Minister: Drugs, alcohol, sexual promiscuity, pornography, and AIDS are just some of the problems youth tell me they are facing. It is sad that even suicide appears to some as an acceptable solution. I believe youth need to learn how to apply biblical principles to their lives. I feel called to help them in that process.

Every thoughtful observer of the modern youth culture is familiar with many of the feelings behind these common expressions of concern. However, the chaotic changes begun in the 1960s, 1970s, and 1980s, as well as the uncertainties and new pressures of the 1990s which have helped to intensify the implications for a youth culture which both exists and is still developing. The contrasts can be seen by comparing some of the problems of high school youth in the 1940s and 1980s.[1]

School Discipline Problems 1940s	Problems of Youth 1980s
Excessive Talking	Alcohol
Chewing Gum	Drugs
Dress Code Violations	Suicide
Cutting in Line	Parents/families
Making Noise	Pregnancy
Running in Hallways	Truancy

Youth sometimes feel that parents and adults do not or cannot clearly understand the problems, realities, anxieties, and stresses of "growing up" today. Some become convinced that adults do not *care* enough to help them cope with pressures created by the temptations and ambiguities of living through the teen years. Feelings of alienation, loneliness, and attempted (and sometimes completed) suicide have often resulted.

Responsible and sincere parents search for "answers" in their parenting roles. Concern for their children often leads them to enroll in parenting seminars and to seek advice from psychologists. As always there have been "experts" waiting to correct and guide them, often with ever-changing theories and advice.[2]

Parenting frustration led one mother to muse: "If you could just bury them at twelve and dig them up at eighteen!" Still another, overhearing but not understanding all her teenager's language, wrote:

> I do not dig this teenage prose.
> Its inner meaning I suppose
> Is what it was when I was young;
> But they don't sling the slang I slung![3]

Parental concerns have intensified with the rise in availability, use, and frequent addiction to alcohol and drugs among youth of America as well as other nations. Teen marriages and pregnancies (often unwanted or for the wrong reasons), venereal diseases, AIDS, abortions, high school dropout rates, runaways (one million a year), and delinquency are other sources of stress and conflict for parents of youth.

Not to be overlooked, of course, are the majority of parents whose youth appear to be well-adjusted, happy, and "normal." Even in some of these cases parents have developed a kind of paranoiac concern over whether their daughter or son has "hidden problems" which should be unmasked and dealt with in a "healthy manner." Eda J. LeShan's called her book *How to Survive Parenthood* and entitled one chapter "The Guilty Parent and How He Grew."[4]

Lay and professional youth leaders often recognize and are concerned about the many problems being experienced among youth. Through personal contact, study groups, reading, retreats, trips, and many other ways these leaders attempt to lead youth into serious and constructive dealings with the "issues" of their lives. This can be a discouraging task. More than a few leaders use words like:

> The kids in my youth group just want to play and have fun. They are not willing to engage in serious study or grapple with tough issues. I wish I could lead them to deal more openly with the nitty-gritty problems they, and we, are facing in today's world. I really want to help equip them with

some coping skills *before* any crises arise instead of trying later to pick up the pieces of troubled or broken lives.

Volunteer lay leaders and staff ministers who work with church youth know themselves to be Christian ministers whose work is grounded in the Bible as the basic resource and guide for living. For them, helping youth involves more than discovering pragmatic ways to face and deal with life's demands. Their special work is to guide youth to discover and apply biblical truths to their task of life-building and serving the living Christ. Ministry thus becomes the sensitive art of learning to yield to the guidance of the Holy Spirit in order to learn how best to live life as a Christian.

In order to help youth meet their special needs, parents, lay leaders, and youth ministers need to construct and utilize a broad spectrum of educational strategies and methods. These include methods such as question-and-answer, discussion, role-play, drama, buzz groups, lecture, videos, computer games, and so forth. Many of these have been presented in the literature for "youth programs."

This book, however, presents an approach to learning which has rarely been developed *systematically* and utilized in working with youth. It is the *case method*, an approach with enables youth, parents, and leaders to grapple with the ambiguities of life and to discover grace through the experiences of people like themselves.

Case Studies and the Bible

The origin of the case method or case study (at least in embryo form) as stories, myths, folk tales, games, anecdotes, and so forth cannot be pinpointed. It is surely as old as the first efforts of primitive parents to entertain or instruct their children. It is clearly found in the more modern "cases" of Little Red Riding Hood, Snow White, Cinderella, Humpty-Dumpty, and countless other familiar children's stories.

The Bible contains many types of case studies. Nathan used a classic story in confronting David about Bathsheba (2 Sam. 12:1-4). There is discussion, questioning, response, and Nathan's sharp application: "[Behold] thou art the man" (v. 7). Such a dialectical approach was carefully formed and utilized by teachers in the rabbinic tradition. "Especially did eminent rabbis (Gamaliel and Hillel) before and in the time of Christ use it freely."[5] For example, rabbis would ask, "What does God do during the fourth quarter of the day?" After discussion, the answer was: "He sits and instructs the school children."[6]

In the best rabbinic tradition, therefore, Jesus refined and used the case study as an effective way to draw His hearers into dialogue, both with Him and one another, regarding life issues such as use of one's talents (Matt. 25:14-30), family relationships (Luke 15:11-32), justice (16:1-15), and forgiveness (Matt. 18:23-35). Who can fail to ponder and learn from His case study which begins with "A certain man [was going] down from Jerusalem to Jericho . . . ." and asks: "Which now of these three, thinkest thou, was neighbor unto him that fell among the thieves?" (Luke 10:30-37).

Called a parable ("to set side by side"), the technique describes human situations and "hooks" hearers into examining the moral principles and spiritual truths which they raise. Jesus even made Himself into a form of "case study" for learning when He asked the disciples "Whom do men say that I am?" and guided the thinking of His followers towards a valid response (Matt.16:13-20).

The Narrative in Biblical Interpretation

Recent developments in biblical interpretation underscore the validity of case studies as an important means for biblical scholarship and the study of Christian theology. Theologian James William McClendon, for example, contends that "the only relevant critical examination of Christian beliefs may be one which attends to lived lives."[7] He argues that by studying the biographies (cases) of persons a theology which accounts for their lives can be discovered. Christian beliefs thus become not so many "theological propositions" but living convictions which give shape to actual lives and actual human communities.

Beginning with the Gospels, John S. Dunn has suggested likewise that autobiography and biography in Scripture provide guidelines for right or Christian living. For Dunn, the shape of reality can best be found in the life-stories of the faithful (in case studies, if you will).[8]

The method of biblical interpretation has recently shifted from the traditional attempts to uncover the meaning of texts by reducing them to their smallest units to an emphasis on and valuing of the basic narrative quality of the texts. Along with this shift of focus regarding the basic text has come a corresponding shift regarding the locus of the text's meaning. Interpreters now hold that rather than being "locked in" the text itself, the real meaning of Scripture is only actualized within the experience of those who study the text, extracting meaning as it is dictated by the basic narrative quality of the text.[9] Thus, a vital source of meaning for Christian living lies in an examination of the life stories of biblical persons (again, case studies).

In his faculty address, New Testament scholar R. Alan Culpepper described how this use of narrative story (or case study) can be seen in the New Testament.

Within this literary context, the author unfolds the story of Jesus in such a way that the reader is led to make various responses and perform a variety of cognitive and emotional tasks in the course of reading the gospel. . . . At points the reader is told what to expect later in the story, or events narrated earlier are recalled. The effect is that the reader moving through the narrative from beginning to end does not move smoothly through the story or story time but is led by the narrator to view the action from different temporal perspectives, with information the characters do not share. . . . From the vantage point of the narrator we watch the characters utter truths unknowingly, condemn themselves unintentionally, and mistake Jesus' identity while claiming knowledge.[10]

Case Studies and Youth Ministry

The case studies in this volume center on the lives of youth and include background material as well as teaching suggestions. It must be pointed out that they have a distinctive characteristic: They are all true cases involving real people. Unlike parables, illustrations, stories, or anecdotes, they are genuine presentations of issues and problems encountered by specific persons. Only minor events and dialogue been edited. Material for each case was supplied by participants in the events who have provided releases for the cases to be used as the record of their recollections and understandings of the events. The authenticity of these cases make them vibrantly alive with reality, true conflict, and decision points.

The purpose of each case is not to illustrate a specific viewpoint or to pass judgment on the actions of others. Rather, each case presents a "slice of life" in which real persons deal with problems and issues common to our human condition. There is no assumption of a superiority which knows "the right answer," for that is not the way we deal with the difficult problems of our lives. Each case should be received, therefore, as a vehicle for examining complexities and ambiguities of our own lives through the experiences of other persons as they cope with their humanness, who "[hath been] in all points tempted like as we are" (Heb. 4:15). It is an evidentiary technique for learning.

Cases are powerful aids for the process; Ross Snyder calls them "theologizing about existence." Snyder quotes Justice Holmes's advice: "We must participate in the passion and action of our times, at peril otherwise of being judged not to have lived."[11] Cases demonstrate the need to translate the theory of books, lectures, and classroom into practice—our theology into *praxis*. As one participant at the Graduate School of Business at Harvard said about the case method:

A student of business with tact
Absorbed many answers he lacked

But acquiring a job,
He said with a sob,
"How *does* one fit answer to fact?"[12]

Youth are often pictured as lacking commitment, as having no burning goals for their lives beyond perhaps that of making money. When well-presented and guided, good case studies beckon learners toward commitment. Both leaders and group members are asked to "put their weight down," to say "this is where I stand on these issues, and here is what I think ought to be done about them." There is a kind of centripetal force in cases which draws persons ever so gently into the circle of discussion and involvement, which makes it difficult for them to play the role of spectator or coach. They become players on the field.

This centripetal effect creates an environment in which learners project themselves into the case. Such projective techniques have long been used to aid insight by stimulating responses without directly asking an individual to do so. The process assumes that the response generated by the stimulus reflects the person's underlying personality, attitudes, and values. Two of the most common projective measures used by psychologists in clinical diagnosis are the Rorschach Inkblot Test and the Thematic Apperception Test (TAT). In the Rorschach Inkblot Test the stimulus is provided by a series of ink blots that are shown the person. The TAT is a series of pictures for which the person makes up stories (what has been happening here, what is going to happen, and so forth).[13] Though the intent is different, teaching-learning through case studies brings some of the values of this process youth discussants of a case.

Let it be said that no claim is made here that this volume is the first or original effort to provide cases for working with youth. For example, in 1953 John W. M. Rothney published such a text for use in training public school teachers. His cases provided school and personal data, along with academic records on pupils for study and evaluation by persons preparing for the teaching profession. However, the cases were not designed or intended for group study by nonprofessionals.[14] Another example is the 1969 publication *Woe is Me!: Case Studies in Moral Dilemmas* which contained cases by nine contributors. Designed to train youth to deal with controversy through discussion, the "cases," however, were admittedly an attempt "to construct open-ended situations in which the solution must be determined by the study group" rather than presenting actual life situations.

Four reasons cited for using case studies in the 1969 publication are:

1. No one can prepare a packaged solution for another person's difficulties.
2. Case studies move us from being overly idealistic and theoretical to an approach which is more nearly "real life" situations.
3. Case studies permit group discussion in problem-solving and group discussion "forces us to be more honest and more thorough in our problem solving techniques."
4. Case studies linger in our minds as object lessons which can help us to be more effective in our everyday problem-solving. Group discussion of specific situations can give us practice and experience in the process of solving personal dilemmas and in applying the ethical teachings of Christ to our lives.[15]

Some Theological Considerations

The intentional introduction of theological considerations into actual life situations presupposes some rationale or foundation. What assumptions about the spiritual dimensions of human life can serve as legitimate premises for the case method approach to learning? Four appear to be foundational.

First, religious experience always precedes the written record of that experience. Indeed, in a real sense the written record is actually a secondary source. God was experienced by persons whose experiences were recorded later in the Bible. The experiencing person was truly the primary source. The events were probably shared orally before being written down, becoming an orally transmitted record. Examples of this are found in stories like those of Luke 15:11-32 and 16:1-8; the encounters of Paul at Jerusalem and the later description of them in Acts 15; the record of 1 Corinthians 12 and 13; and the appealing events described by Paul in Philemon.

The best and most helpful insights often come to us through an experiencing person(s) in a life event. The best case studies thus are the written record of the experiences which have been shared by the person(s) who have "lived through" (and may still be "living through" them at the time) the events described. Case studies in this book are of this type.

Second, religious experience and understanding are always developmental before being presented systematically. The Bible traces how God revealed Himself to human beings and how the oral transmission of those experiences came to be a kind of "systematic theology" in written form. God expects us to use our minds as we attempt to understand and develop our more systematic statements about His revelation. It is not coincidental that Jesus' first commandment includes the provision that "thou shalt love the Lord thy God . . . with all thy mind" (Mark 12:30).

Such a developmental view suggests that our life stages impact and shape our needs and help to focus ways in which theology can be most helpful in meeting them. Case studies assist discussants to enter vicariously into the experiences of other persons and thereby examine, clarify, and judge the validity of their own views.

Third, problem solving is the primary method through which persons encounter and consider making decisions about the gospel of Jesus Christ. In fact, the epistles of the New Testament are letters written usually with the purpose of helping believers solve problems and address specific life needs rather than to serve as theological treatises, which they became only later. A great deal of other parts of the Bible serve the same purpose, that of problem solving. Likewise, case studies present experiences from the lives of others which can be important aids for examining issues and actions in our own lives. Therefore, it is not surprising that Dr. Krister Stendahl, then Professor of New Testament at Harvard Divinity School, observed that "the Bible is actually a casebook."[16]

Fourth, nurturing and educating persons in faith is most effective when it focuses on life needs rather than on theoretical or contrived data. Life's problems and concerns are the "case studies" which beckon the believer to "theologize about existence." They create the continuing interest and dynamic which make the adventure of living so exciting and deliver us from ennui. It is from within the framework of these "mysteries" of life that preaching, doctrine, Bible study, church ordinances, and religious truth are needed, become meaningful, and "make sense" to us.

Case studies also enable us to examine and affirm the complexities of life against our desire to possess psychometrically tested "right answers." In reality human life is a series of events which must be lived through as well as examined and accepted. Further, we are often forced to choose an action which is only one among several good possibilities. Experience teaches us that we often must also decide without having all the information and facts for which we long. That's life and so are the cases which follow.

Part 2
Case Studies

1

Ron Scanlon, Teenager

Ron Scanlon was a nice-looking, upper middle-class fifteen-year-old. His slight build, curly hair, general appearance, and ready friendliness belied his youth. Although not quick to smile, his fine features and sense of confidence suggested an openness to social interaction. Handshaking, which was accomplished with minimal awkwardness and casual conversation even with a stranger, seemed easy for Ron as he began an interview which had been requested by the author and arranged by Ann Jacobs, minister of youth at the church where Ron was a member of the youth group. The verbatim of the interview follows.

"I was born in Arlington, Virginia. My parents had each been divorced previously, and I have an older half-brother (nine years older) by my father's first marriage. I come from a strong background. My grandparents are strong believers and active in church. I lived my first seven years in Maryland.

"I had an older brother named Jimmy who was really wild, taking drugs, being rowdy, ripping off cars, and so forth. At fifteen he was really doing some crazy stunts. Jimmy never liked my mom. He and my dad never got along well either. He and my dad fought a lot since Dad felt he could keep him in line by physically controlling him. It didn't work though because he was on probation a lot. Jimmy is about twenty-four now, I think.

"I also had a little brother named Mark, but he died when I was four. So until then certain things had been in my life, you know, hard things like that.

"My father was transferred when I was about eight, and we moved to Florida. We lived in an apartment at first. I had some friends and, uh, my friends were always kinda mean towards me. I wasn't very popular. I used to get picked on a lot.

"When I was thirteen, we bought an expensive, new house. Up until that time my life had been kinda boring, so I was trying to pick it up. I had two best friends, Gene and Roger. We were really tight, you know. Then suddenly certain things were happening, and they weren't my

19

best friends anymore. Sometimes that happens with your friends, so I made new friends.

"About this time my parents were having lots of problems. One day they called me in. They were sitting on the couch and told me everything. About six months later, they divorced. I decided to live with my dad. We moved into a small, two-bedroom condominium, and my mom moved to St. Louis. My dad and I fixed a lot of things in the condominium—shingles, paint, and so forth. Problems started happening between us. You know, money is the root of all evil. Well, that's what I think it was based on. I didn't think I had enough money ($40.00 every two weeks). We started arguing about things like who was taking care of what parts of the house, you know, problems that go along with living with each other. Certain people called us the 'odd couple' because he was really neat and I was the sloppy kid [nervous laugh]. It's still the same way, I guess.

"About a year later my Dad wanted to make an investment so he bought a bigger condominium about two blocks away from here, and that's where I'm living now. It's bigger. We moved in last summer, about eight months ago. When we first moved, I met a girl named Carol. I was really in love but now I don't think I was. I liked her, and I kept trying to persuade her to date me. We became really close friends. She was my girlfriend for about four days, and then she broke up with me and started going with one of my friends, Rich, who was seventeen and out of school.

"Up until this time I had not been in real trouble. I had no record and was a pretty mellow guy. Rich had these friends: Tim, Tom, and Butterball. They would go out with high-powered BB guns, pistols, slingshots, and rocks, and knock over houses, and they wanted me to go with them. I knew what they were doing. (Now that I'm older and look back on it, it was stupid. I've done a lot of stupid things.) It was last December, and I was drunk. They rode around, would take a pistol, and shoot out the window in a car—a whole bunch of cars and houses, too. They would shoot anything that would break. They never shot people. They shot out the windows of a movie theater. I was having a great time, laughing my head off. . . . I thought it was funny. I was pretty high on beer and pot. We stopped at a chain of flashing lights around a ditch in the street, and I jumped out, smashed twelve of them with a club, and took off. They took me home. The next night I went out and did it again and had a great time. There was a whole gang of kids that got into it—I don't even know them all. I'll bet you read about it in the paper.

"About a week later a cop came to Rich's door. Somebody had told on everybody—except me. It was a girl who was in the car. She was scared because it was a felony offense and didn't want any part of it. She didn't know my name because I was only with them the last two days and they had been doing this for over ten straight days. She just knew my name was Ron.

"Rich got a court summons and was tried as a minor. Rich and I are still good friends. Tim and Tom told on the fourteen to fifteen others involved—everybody but me because they didn't know my full name either. The cops never found out! By the way, my dad doesn't know anything about it yet. Tim, Tom, and Butterball were all over eighteen and were tried as adults.

"A few days later I met a fifteen-year-old named Bob at school. Rich, Bob, and I were all good friends, partying together. By this time Carol and Rich weren't dating anymore. Bob and Carol were giving each other the eye and 'bam' they were going together. I was upset and jealous of Bob. I was infuriated. I was so mad. I used to give him dirty looks all the time.

"Rich, Bob, and I continued to party together, which meant alcohol and drugs. Then one day Bob and Rich spotted a silver Mercedes in a parking lot running with the door open. Bob said, 'Come on, Rich, let's jump in and take it for a ride.' Rich didn't want to go at first, but Bob finally talked him into it.

"They came to my house about 3:30 p.m. Rich ran up to the door saying, 'Ron, Ron, we got a Mercedes from a parking lot. Let's go!' I ran all the way to the car and jumped in the back of the two-seater.

"When you're in a stolen car you don't want to make yourself noticeable, right? Well, Bob was driving behind a VW, speeded up to pass it, and barely missed a truck which was coming head-on. It scared me half to death! He was doing about 120 m.p.h., and a cop saw us. We outran him, but then we were passing a park which is a teenage hangout, and Bob turns in. We protested, but Bob insisted he wanted to show the car off. He drove right by a cop, and he came after us. I was terrified. We went over 100 m.p.h. down a winding road and took a corner at 60 m.p.h. When we did that, Bob blew it, and we ran into a parked El Camino, with the cop right on us. Bob yelled for us to run; and we did, but the cop circled around and suddenly was in front of us, pistol drawn, shouting: 'Freeze, partner!' He made us spread-eagle on the sidewalk. Almost immediately other cars arrived, including the K-9 patrol. Five cops had their guns on three teenagers. They were filming the arrest and the El Camino owner was busily taking pictures of it all. They put handcuffs on us that hurt.

"They kept us separated and interrogated us at the jail. Bob decided to tell them everything—just what a cop would love to hear. Another cop came to me and said, 'Your friend just spilled the whole story.' So I told the story so it would get me off easier. Rich remained silent and insisted on seeing a lawyer.

"When we appeared in court, the judge looked at Bob and said: 'I don't like rip-offs, and *I don't like you.*' I was given eight weekend work details and probation for six months; Bob got eleven work details and six months of probation. Further, we were told not to see each other again, refrain from alcohol and drugs, obey our parents, and observe a curfew of 10:00 p.m. weeknights and 1:00 a.m. on Fridays and Saturdays. That was different from all-night partying I did before I got caught for this. That happened four weeks ago.

"I don't care what the Probation Department says; they can't pick your friends for you. Bob, Rich, and I are friends. There are no hard feelings between us, and we are still seeing one another. Also, I have still been doing drugs. The last time I took something was at a concert two weeks ago. I'm not planning to do it again.

"My friend Rich was tried for the earlier vandalism. My dad didn't like Rich because he was out of school and all. Dad tried restrict me from leaving the house. He tried to enforce it physically. One day Rich was at my house, and my dad tried to keep me from leaving by putting me in a headlock. Rich knocked my dad into a wall, and Rich and I were ready to take him on. He ordered Rich to leave before he called the cops. I left with him and moved in with Rich for about a week. I'm really close to Rich's parents.

"Then I stayed with Chris's mom. (Chris is in the youth group here.) They live right next door to my dad. I hadn't been home for nine days, and Chris's mom urged me to visit. My dad and I started arguing, and I started cursing. He nailed me right in the left eye [chuckle] and then in the right eye [chuckle]. I tried to fight back; and I knocked out one of his teeth, but he killed me. There's no doubt about it that he could pulverize me. I left and went back with my black eyes to Chris's mother (who wanted me to leave by now). She said, 'Oh, my God, look at what I sent you home to!' Then she wanted me to stay.

"For a long time now I have had all these problems piling up on me— the Youth Crisis Center, police after me, and so forth. I worried about my problems. Where will I eat? Where's my money coming from? Where will I sleep? Where will I get everything?

"Right now I'm trying to straighten out my life. I have *A*'s in three subjects: biology, physical education, and creative writing. I wrote a ten-page story called 'Crystals,' a space-type thing, and got an *A* on it. I have a *C* plus in math; I'm coming up there.

"I'm still smoking pot but less frequently. My tolerance for pot has gone down. I'm still drinking; I had a case last night with some friends at my house. My dad's out of town on a ski trip so I had the house to myself. I have about $600 in the bank but my dad is holding it until I am more responsible. I'm looking for a part-time job.

"Things are better with my dad—we're talking more. Don't get the idea that I'm the bad guy and dad is all good. He's got problems, too. He goes to bars every night. I don't think he's an alcoholic, but I've seen him drunk many times. When I came in totally stoned on drugs and alcohol one night, all he said was 'Wow! Your eyes are really red.' (Red eyes are a symptom of being stoned, you know.)"

At this point Ron paused and said, "OK, now what do you think?"

The author responded: "I am impressed that you are an intelligent young man. You seem to have a good ability to articulate what you experience and feel. You are capable and appear to be maturing. You're smart."

Ron interrupted and replied: "You know something. I'd be smarter if I didn't take any drugs [chuckle]. I've stopped taking LSD. LSD is acid in the true sense. It fries, you know, it melts things. Goes right to your brain cells. I'm not going to take it again [chuckle]. Its not addictive or anything; its just a great high.

"I think you have a good idea, more than what anybody else does, of what's been the problem with me."

Ponderings for Pedagogy

This case helps us to think about one specific youth, Ron Scanlon. It presents no "flash point" at which the person has arrived and which demands some immediate action. Instead, it is one person's effort to really listen to and "hear" one individual youth. This technique, called *conversational research* by psychologist Thomas Cottle, contrasts our tendency to be too theoretical or to fail to listen to each young person. It helps counter the charge by some youth that "no one ever listens to me!"

A major problem in understanding youth lies in the area of research about them. Joseph Adelson, nationally respected researcher on adolescence and professor of psychology and director of the psychological clinic at the University of Michigan, has argued that many common perceptions about youth do not reflect reality. This is because research on adolescence is meager in quantity and the data is "soft." Further, he reports too much of what has been done has focused on atypical youth, sometimes even consisting solely of a population which was institutionalized. Research has therefore tended to include and/or focus principally on youth who were not coping well and were trying to discover and remedy what was missing in their lives.[1]

Adelson found that general theories of adolescence were therefore unwittingly based on small and atypical youth samples. For example, small amounts of data have been generated about adolescent girls, a fact which has skewed studies toward adolescent males. In addition, many important topics in adolescent psychology have been omitted or inadequately addressed. (For example, little is known about their rational thought processes, coping and adaptation processes, or normal religious expressions of the young).[2]

Two examples of misconceptions about youth are the "generation gap" and national elections. It was widely assumed that society was polarized in the 1960s. Research disclosed, however, that no more division by age existed in another historical period. All strata of American society, not only youth, were affected at that time by the significant changes in politics and values. The important divisions were (and are) not basically generational but have far more to do with social class, education, economics, race, and religious background.

As to politics, in 1972 conventional wisdom about youth indicated that eighteen-year-olds would exercise their newly acquired right to vote, transform American politics, and elect George M. McGovern. They didn't. In 1988 pollsters believed youth would support Michael Dukakis. Again, they did not, many of them did not bother to vote. Such information led Adelson to conclude that:"Taken as a whole, adolescents are *not* in turmoil, *not* deeply disturbed, *not* at the mercy of their impulses, *not* resistant to parental values, *not* politically active, and *not* rebellious."[3] In a similar reaction, Professor Amitai Etzioni of Columbia University arrived at another significant conclusion.

> Yet the only solid generalization that emerges from nationwide studies of voting behavior, attitudes, values, and opinions is that the term "youth" ought to be banned as a meaningless abstraction. Americans under 30 vary immensely and have rather little in common.[4]

Perhaps these are among the reasons David Elkind, chairman of the Eliot Pearson Department of Child Study and professor at Tufts University, believes that today's adolescents are "unplaced" in American society.[5] Like babies whose parents are waving flashcards of the alphabet in their infants' faces before age one, adolescents are pressured to achieve more at an earlier age—academically, socially, and sexually. The result is a fear of failure, a suspicion that society's promises to them for the future are not being kept, and an uneasy feeling that "I don't know how I fit in." Indeed, Elkind says: "There is no place for teenagers in American society today—not in our homes, not in our schools, and not in our society at large."[6]

Another area of misinformation is the rate and effect of divorce upon children. Growth in the divorce rate is not as great as is often assumed. Divorce rates have increased as follows: 1880—one in twenty-one marriages; 1900—one in twelve; 1916—one in nine; 1979—one in three.[7] However, in 1987 pollster Louis Harris reported that only one in eight marriages now end in divorce and in any single year only about 2 percent of marriages (1.2 million) break up while "a much, much bigger 54 million other marriages just keep flowing along." He concludes "that the American family is surviving under enormous pressure."[8]

The effect of divorce upon children and youth is of great concern to parents and those in helping professions. Divorced parents report deterioration of their parenting skills lasting as much as two years after the breakup. They later recover their parenting skills but usually have refined them. The older a youngster is at the time of their parents' divorce the more success they display in coping with its effects.[9]

Some findings from a study by R. A. Kulka and H. Weingarten on the long-term effects experienced by *adults* whose parents divorced when they were young are:

1. Such adults reported their youth as the most unhappy time of their lives.
2. They do not report greater levels of unhappiness, worry, or anxiety about the future.
3. They tend to report more marital dissatisfaction and have a higher incidence of separation or divorce than do adults from intact homes.[10]

Further, some implication for Ron Scanlon may be reflected in a series of studies on the effects of the loss of the father rather than the mother through divorce which found that children in that event have lower levels of self-esteem than those from nondivorced homes.[11]

A Case Time Line

Since more than a dozen persons are mentioned, begin your study of the case by writing the names and identifying each one. Think about the relationship of each to Ron Scanlon and the total case presentation. Since a considerable time span is involved, it would also be wise to trace the events chronologically. The following time line illustrates this recommended procedure both for this case and the others which follow.

Time-Event Sequence

(1) *Born*
Arlington, Virgina
Parents each previously divorced
Half brother (nine years older) by father's first marriage
Strong Christian background

Grandparents are strong believers; active in church

(2) *First Seven Years*
Lived in Maryland.
Older brother Jimmy is rowdy and steals cars. He and Dad did not get along. He never really liked my mom. Dad used physical control. Jimmy on probation a lot.
Mark died when Ron was four.

(3) *Eight Years Old*
Moved to Florida
Friends: "Mean towards me . . . picked on a lot"

(4) *Thirteen Years Old*
Expensive house. Life "boring." Two friends: Gene and Roger "real tight." "Suddenly certain things were happening, and they weren't my best friends anymore." Parents divorced. "I was really upset." Dad in two-bedroom condo. Mom moved to St. Louis. Worked on condo and divided chores. Argued over allowance of $40 every two weeks. Called "odd couple."

(5) *About Fourteen*
Dad invested in a second condo. Lived there about eight months now. Met Carol: "Really in love, but I don't think I was." She went with Ron for four days, broke up, and went with Ron's friend, Rich.

(6) *About Fifteen*
Rich had friends named Tim, Tom, and Butterball (all over eighteen). Last December they shot out and threw rocks through car windows, houses, and a movie theater for a period of about ten days. Flashing lights on ditch with club. Girl told on everybody "except me (didn't know my name)."

(7) *Later*
Partying with Rich and Bob: Alcohol and drugs.
Bob and Rich stole Mercedes; picked up Ron about 3:30 p.m. Police chased up to 120 m.p.h., hit El Camino, caught
Bob told everything " . . . just what a cop would love to hear"; Ron talked; Rich demanded a lawyer

(8) *In Court*
Judge to Bob, "I don't like ripoffs and *I don't like you*
Bob: Eleven weekend work details and six months probation.
Ron: Eight weekend work details and six months probation.
Told not to see each other again; curfew, 10:00 p.m. weeknights and 1:00 a.m. Fridays and Saturdays. "This was four weeks ago."

(9) *Ron*
Still doing drugs; last time at a concert two weeks ago. "I'm not planning to do it again"
Rich arrested for vandalism
Ron moved in with Rich ("I'm really close to Rich's parents")

Moved in with Chris's mom (Chris in youth group here.)
(Got two black eyes; knocked out Dad's tooth)

(10) *Straightening Out*
School: A in three classes this month. Creative writing on "Crystals," a space thing and got A. Some pot, but less. Dad is holding $600 of my money. Allowance is $40.00/two weeks. "Things are better with Dad . . . we're talking more . . . " "I think you have a good idea, more than what anybody else does, of what's been the problem with me."

Most persons find that identifying the "actors" helps to relate and interpret the events.

Group Leadership

Discussion uses the reactions and perceptions of one youth to examine some needs and possibilities in youth ministry. This case lends itself to worker training, parent meetings, parent-youth dialogue, and trialogues for parent-youth-workers. It could also be used to introduce a series of studies on issues in adolescence.

Using your knowledge about the group, develop a general plan for leading group study. A sequence of possible questions is most often the best approach. Begin by having group members identify each person in the case, along with pertinent information about each individual. Use the following steps in preparing for the study.

• On a chalkboard, newsprint, or overhead projector, place a chart which represents Ron's development in five areas—physically, morally, socially, intellectually, and religiously. Use this chart following the discussion of the persons in the case.

Ask: How would you rate Ron's development physically, morally, socially, intellectually, and religiously? Record the responses by using a heavy dot for each judgment of the group. Do you feel any of our judgments about these are especially significant? What implications can you see for each score?

- What needs do you think Ron is seeking to meet or fulfill? (Record.) What is Ron seeking in life? Are these "typical" concerns among youth? Consider using the information given in the following *Needs of Youth* section and asking: Are these needs which Ron is working on? Which ones? How? Evidence? Progress toward them?

- Can you see any patterns in Ron's life? Some possibilities could be temporary relationships, conflict, rejection, disappointments, inadequate supervision, or poor adult role models. Others? What do you think Ron means by saying: what's been the problem with me?

- What do you feel Ron is *really* doing or attempting when he "was having a great time" breaking windows and flashing lights? What was its *function* for him (anger, belonging, alcohol, prestige)? Could it have been "fun" for him? Why? Over 2,000,000 traffic signs are vandalized and must be replaced each year in the U.S. at a cost of over $100,000,000 per year.

- Why do you suppose Ron chose to live with his father with whom he seemed to be in so much conflict? Why didn't he decide to live with his mother in St. Louis? How would you typify the role of the father in Ron's life (provider, model, instability, distant, or other)?

- Give a summary of the stages of moral development suggested by Lawrence Kohlberg of Harvard University (see below). Ask: Using this assessment technique, where would you place Ron? Why? Ask them to cite specific data for their suggestions. (Most researchers would probably place Ron at "Preconventional Level, Stage 2.")

- How would you respond to this statement: "In most respects Ron Scanlon is a typical teenager. He is simply trying to meet his needs in his own way." After response, ask in what ways is Ron typical of today's teenager?

- What do you think is the role of the church's minister of youth in Ron's life? Why does Ron continue to relate to church at all? What is its function for him?

- If you could pick up the interview where the author left off, what would you say? What would be your first important question to him? What would you *seek* with and for him? What would you try to *do* for Ron? Would you try to make contact with his father? For what purpose?

- Consider using the form *Who Is a Youth?* found below. Ask each person (silently) to complete the reaction column for each description. Then briefly discuss their feelings about the adequacy of each. Discuss their definitions. Emphasis should be given to the uniqueness of every person. This form could also be used as the activity to *begin* the discussion.

The discussion should produce a generous supply of *implications* about youth, parents, adult workers with youth, and responsibilities of the group who is discussing the case. Some time may be reserved for specifying and judging the importance of these.

There are resources for grace. Believing in God enables a person to search for His presence in life. When it is recognized and appropriated, God's grace (literally, "things freely given") abounds in human experiences. Where are the locations of grace for Ron Scanlon? Do the potential sources of grace include persons such as Chris's mother? The minister of youth? School teachers? Friends? Other sources?

Needs of Youth

Needs of youth, as discussed in current literature, represent an amorphous collection which may be classified as (1) psychological statements, (2) tasks, (3) problems, (4) wants or wishes, or (5) adjustments required by one's societal context. Donald Doane observed, "Statements of the needs and problems of youth vary as widely as the philosophies of those presenting them and as the means by which the statements are formulated."[12]

The following statements of need are suggested as a list of "working statements."

1. Youth need to make consistent progress in balancing support and independence from parents and other adults.
2. Youth need to understand and accept their physical characteristics and appropriate sex roles.
3. Youth need reliable information and guidance for the process of making occupational choices consistent with interests, abilities, and self-fulfillment.
4. Youth need guidance in developing behavior which aids peer acceptance, social competence, and civic participation.
5. Due to growth in their mental abilities, youth need freedom to develop an intellectually defensible religious faith which can provide hope for meeting life's problems and a feeling of personal security.
6. Youth need a moral system which can guide ethical thinking and behavior.
7. From the Christian perspective, youth need opportunities to accept Jesus Christ as Savior and Lord, respond to Him in personal faith, and become growing Christian disciples.

Kohlberg's Stages of Moral Development

Lawrence Kohlberg describes three levels in the development of moral character. These are given here in generalized and abbreviated form.

I. Preconventional Level (Premoral)

Stage 1: Punishment and obedience orientation. Physical consequences of action determine its goodness or badness regardless of human meaning or value of these consequences.

Stage 2: Instrumental relativist orientation. Right action consists of that which instrumentally satisfies one's own needs and the needs of others in the situation.

II. Conventional Level

Stage 3: Interpersonal concordance or "good boy-nice girl" orientation. Good behavior is what pleases or helps others and is approved by them. There is much conformity to stereotypical images of what is majority or "natural" behavior.

Stage 4: The law and order orientation. Orientation toward authority, fixed rules, and the maintenance of social order.

III. Postconventional, Autonomous, or Principles Level

Stage 5: Social-contract, legalistic orientation. Emphasis upon the legal view of right conduct.

Stage 6: Universal ethical-principle orientation. Right is the decision of conscience based upon self-chosen ethical principles which appeal to logical comprehensiveness, universality, and consistency (The Golden Rule, the categorical imperative).

Who Is a Youth?

Field	*Description*	*Reaction?*
1. Education	A person who is completing mandatory schooling.	
2. Economic	A person who is dependent on parents for financial support.	
3. Culture	A person who is passing through mandated rites of passage to adulthood.	
4. Social	A person whose reference group is teenagers.	
5. Biological	A person who is capable of sexual reproduction.	
6. Psychological	A person who has not yet cut the psychological umbilical cord that united the person to the family of origin (or) a person not yet capable of mature decision making.	
7. Legal	A person who has not reached the age of majority as deter-	

8. Physiological

       mined by legal authority.
A person whose synaptic structure (brain connectivity) has not yet reached maturation.

9. Dictionary

       "Quality or state of being young. The part of life that succeeds childhood."

Complete:

       "A youth is_____

_____

_____ ."

Suggested Resources

Aleshire, Dan. *Understanding Today's Youth*. Nashville: Convention Press, 1982.

Blackburn, Bill, and Blackburn, Deana Mattingly. *Caring in Times of Family Crisis*. Nashville: Convention Press, 1987.

Campolo, Anthony. *Growing Up in America*. Grand Rapids: Zondervan Publishing Co., 1989.

Strommen, Merton. *Five Cries of Youth*. Rev. Ed. San Francisco: Harper and Row, 1988.

2

A Trip to Six Flags

Warren Stevens (A)[1]

Warren Stevens was just beginning to relax and enjoy the day at Six Flags Over Georgia when he heard his name blaring over the public address system. It had taken a lot of planning to get his youth group to Atlanta for the day. Warren was serving as the summer minister of youth at Saluda Baptist Church in Anderson, South Carolina. He had just completed his first year as a seminary student, and he was excited about this chance to put into practice some of the things he had been studying and learning.

When he was paged to come to the courtesy booth, he immediately wondered what had happened. His youth group had been given the freedom to wander around without any of the five chaperons "tagging along." After all, he felt, the youth were not small children who needed someone to keep them from getting lost. Warren believed they had proved to be responsible enough to handle freedom. The group had been instructed to meet at the front park entrance to eat lunch together. The twenty youth included sophomores, juniors, and seniors in high school. All were enrolled in youth Sunday School classes.

Five Chaperons

The five chaperons were Warren, June Lewis, Harold Kotter, Bob and Carol Simmons, and John Pike (the pastor). Mrs. Lewis was an older Sunday School teacher who was well-liked by youth in the Youth I Department and had volunteered to come on the trip "to be with the young people." She was a fairly healthy person, but Warren worried that the trip and mid-July heat might be too much for her. As he continued to walk toward the courtesy booth, he wondered if she had become ill.

Bob and Carol were teachers in the Youth II Department and in their early thirties. They were energetic, and the young people enjoyed being around them. Harold Kotter was a friend of Warren's who had just finished work on his bachelor's degree in music and was unemployed.

Although he was an active member in another church in Anderson, he had helped Warren with several different youth programs during the summer and was well-liked by the youth.

Reverend Pike had also come along; he said "to help chaperon the trip." Warren knew better. He knew that the pastor wanted to go to Six Flags almost as much as the youth, two of whom were his sons. Warren was pleased, but somewhat amused by the pastor's enthusiasm for being with the youth and going to the amusement park. Warren felt Reverend Pike did not seem to relate well with the youth.

The Security Office

Upon arriving at the courtesy booth, Warren saw Reverend Pike already waiting for him.

"What is the problem? Is something wrong?" Warren asked.

Reverend Pike replied, "The park guards want to see us in the security office. That's all I know."

Warren felt his pulse quicken. *Oh no! What could have happened?*' he thought to himself. Warren knew that the youth liked to "cut up" and be a little rowdy, but they were basically good kids and knew when to stop fooling around.

As they entered the security office, Warren noticed one of the boys from the group sitting in a side room looking very dejected. It was Robbie Dowd. Warren did not know what the situation was and, to make matters worse, did not know Robbie very well either.

Robbie was a member of the Sunday School but had not attended much until he heard about the trip to Six Flags. Warren knew that Robbie came from a less-privileged family, and they lived in a small, unkempt-looking house about six blocks from the church. During the summer, Robbie had been working a little with his father, a self-employed handyman. His father had agreed to let him off from work to go on the trip. Robbie seemed to be rather quiet, and the other church youth were known to tease him about his shaggy (sometimes unwashed) hair which hung to his shoulders. Robbie responded to them with a roughness that bordered between good-natured playing around and actual fighting. Usually the matter would pass in a few moments, and no one seemed to think any more about it.

Warren viewed Robbie's coming on this trip as a way to get to know and perhaps to talk with him. He felt that Robbie needed the attention of someone who would make him feel his own worth. Also, Warren hoped that after being with the youth for awhile in this relaxed environment, maybe they would become more accepting of Robbie. Now, however, something else had developed.

Robbie Charged with Shoplifting

Robbie had been caught shoplifting in the park by one of the gift shop clerks. When she questioned him, he started to run away. The woman grabbed his arm, but he took a swing at her with his fist. A security guard nearby arrived and took Robbie into custody. Robbie denied stealing the item, a windup train with "Souvenir of Six Flags Over Georgia" written on it. The guard reported he had taken it from Robbie's pocket. The officer told Warren and Reverend Pike, "We usually press charges against people who threaten our employees, and shoplifting is bad around here so I would have no problem in calling the sheriff to come get him. That might not be the best thing for him in the long run. Since he is with your church group, if he will confess and apologize to our salesperson, I will release him in your custody. That is, if you will take the responsibility to see that he is properly disciplined."

Warren's Decision

Reverend Pike seemed a little bewildered by the incident. Warren, feeling directly responsible for Robbie, asked to speak to him alone in the side room. Trying not to alienate Robbie, Warren asked if he needed some money to pay for the train, explaining that if Robbie would make restitution it might help. Robbie pulled out his wallet, thumbed through some bills. Warren was surprised to see he had over a hundred dollars in it.

This caused Warren to wonder why Robbie had stolen the train. *Why didn't he spend the money? The train only cost $9.95 plus tax. How did he get so much money when his father's business did not appear to be that well off? Maybe if I had tried harder to be with him Robbie would not have done this. How am I going to handle this incident?* Warren thought.

A Trip to Six Flags (B)

Reverend Pike seemed perplexed and somewhat uncertain about what should be done about Robbie's dilemma. A refined college and seminary graduate, Reverend Pike was more comfortable as a biblical expositor than as a crisis counselor.

Warren Stevens had formerly worked in the retail sales business and was not unfamiliar with shoplifting. However, he wanted to avoid a hasty reaction and also wished to maintain a good relationship with Robbie. After a brief consultation, Reverend Pike and Warren agreed to ask Robbie to apologize and pay for the train. Robbie was very noncommittal, mumbling something about "having done it." He refused to apologize. Warren finally decided to pay for the train and give it to Robbie, saying they would work out payment later.

When confronted with Robbie's refusal to apologize and Warren's offer to buy the train, the security guard confessed to Warren that he was bluffing about further prosecution and only wanted to get the kid off his hands. He agreed to release Robbie into the care of Reverend Pike and Warren. Throughout the remainder of the day Warren made certain that Robbie was in the presence of one of them. Fortunately, no other youth knew specifically what had happened. When some youth asked about the call for him over the PA system, Warren smiled and said it was a personal matter.

On returning to Anderson, Warren did not notify Robbie's parents about the incident for fear they would respond harshly. He was never able to discover where the hundred dollars came from, since he felt it was not really his business to interrogate Robbie or his parents about it. He did establish a degree of friendship with Robbie who for awhile actively attended most youth functions at the church, though he did not repay the money for the train.

Reverend Pike made no attempt to counsel with Robbie, leaving that to Warren, and the teenager became less active in the youth program as the summer wore on. As summer ended, Warren thought: *I feel sure that the relationship I have established with him over this short period of time has affected him positively. He needs someone who would be here to work with and understand him, without feeling threatened by that person.* However, the summer was soon over, and it was time for Warren Stevens to return to seminary.

Ponderings for Pedagogy

The motivations or reasons for stealing are numerous and often unclear. S. K. Saltzman quotes a teenager named Jenny: "I liked getting something for nothing—especially things I couldn't afford. In a way it was exciting—like I kept winning a game of chance." He also suggests additional reasons: financial need, impulsive act, acceptance by friends who steal, projects image of being daring and unafraid, and a wish for attention from parents preoccupied with their own problems (financial crisis, divorce, alcoholism).[2] So-called "high society shoplifters" steal rarely out of necessity; most often it is "nonsensical theft" such as the widely publicized department store stealing by former Miss America Bess Myerson. Challenge and low self-esteem have been suggested to be factors in stealing.[3] Attorney Tom Clark, who has represented many youth charged with shoplifting, believes society's tolerant attitudes adds to the problem. He says people are taught not to get caught more than not to steal.[4]

In their chapter "Dishonesty," T. B. Maston and W. M. Pinson include cheating, lying, and stealing as three forms of dishonesty. However, they confess, "When we started out to write this book we did not plan a section on stealing. But a number of young people urged us to include it. They insisted that stealing is widespread among young people."[5]

Saltzman validates this need by reporting that about 5 million teenagers shoplift each year.[6] Shoplifting in 1984 was reported to approximate 8 billion dollars, and 44 percent of which was committed by store employees.[7]

Additionally, stealing in the U.S. annually amounts to more than the projected cost of forty stealth bombers; 2 million Americans are charged each year with shoplifting; 45 percent of shoplifters are female and 55 percent male; and only about 1 percent of shoplifters are kleptomaniacs.[8] Merton Strommen also reported in his landmark 1958-62 study of over 3,000 Lutheran youth that 38 percent admitted to being tempted to steal and 83 percent to cheat.[9] His *Five Cries of Youth*, published in 1988, reported a distinct decline of traditional moral values among youth. For example, in 1985, 80 percent of high school seniors said their classmates would not care if they cheated on a test.[10]

Two additional sources supply disheartening data about greed and stealing among church-related persons. John Baldwin, president of the North American Securities Administrators Association reported that "divinely inspired" investment schemes have fleeced about 15,000 U.S. citizens out of $450 million since 1985. One con artist (now serving a ten-year jail term) stole 18 million dollars from greedy clients. He was treasurer of one of the largest Baptist churches in Alabama at the time.[11] The other data comes from David Barrett, a researcher with the Foreign Mission Board of the Southern Baptist Convention, who estimates the "ecclesiastical crime" of embezzling church funds is done by 5 percent of the world's Christian workers and amounts to $760 million each year![12] Stealing in America is a serious problem which cuts across economic, social, and every other group distinction.

Such data has caused me to ask whether youth can be taught right and wrong in a public school setting. Leaders at Theodore Roosevelt High School in Bronx, New York, believe they can to some extent. A course called "Respect, Care, and Share" addresses broad values thought to be common for all persons. Students report the course makes them aware of at least two sides to issues and encourages them to develop some decision-making approaches to problems. It is significant to note that teachers and educators involved in this effort insist they have found and have identified some basic values which people do agree on such as honesty, fairness (one technique involves a "Fairness Committee" of youth), and right and wrong, even apart from any specific religious teaching or denominational expression.[13] Their effort is a start, not a final answer, but the effort lends hope to the prospect of finding some ways to teach moral behavior in public as well as private schools.

Any temptation to praise the effectiveness of private schools in teaching and securing correct pupil behavior, however, is tempered by studies such as the one conducted by the Youth Research Center for Lutheran Schools and reported by Milo Brekke in *How Different Are People Who Attend Lutheran Schools?* While acknowledging the values and positive impact Lutheran schools make, Brekke concluded:

> The beliefs of those who attend parochial schools are decidedly different. But as far as changed attitudes and different behaviors are concerned, parochial schools demonstrate little impact other than upon worship attendance and certain practices of personal piety. Cognitive impact seems to be greatest, affective less, and behavioral the least, . . . this summary finding raises questions about the depth of the impact. Beliefs are clearly affected, attitudes less so, behaviors very little.[14]

Group Leadership

Youth trips come in many shapes and sizes and include everything from skating parties to eating out to trips which last several days (mission and choir tours). As with longer excursions, one-day trips require good leadership and planning if their purposes are to be achieved. In spite of good planning and preparation having been made, however, no one can be certain of outcomes or ensure there will be no surprises or glitches, like the ones which happened to Warren Stevens during the trip to Six Flags.

Begin the study by asking group members to complete the following crossword puzzle which contains the names of persons in the case and some facts involved. When everyone has finished, give members an opportunity to share answers. This exercise could be done in groups of two to three persons.

As the "answers" are shared, ask how each one fits into the case. What do we know about him, her, the place, the event, and so forth? Write down the words and identifications which are suggested, and discuss this data. Guide the discussion toward a process of identifying

A TRIP TO SIX FLAGS

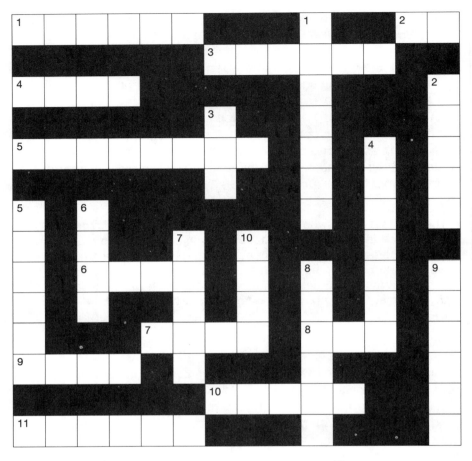

Across

1. Held a surprise for Warren
2. State
3. "Welcome back, _____"
4. First month of summer
5. Church's location
6. Encouragement for the future
7. _____'s Peak
8. Travel by
9. Add "d" to Chemical company
10. Article in question
11. First word in church name

Down

1. State capital
2. _____ Channing
3. _____ Dole, Senator
4. Begins like last name of N.Y. Giants quarterback, Phil _____
5. _____ Arlen, silent film comedian
6. Gospel writer
7. Last name of famous Olympic runner
8. Nickname for Robert
9. _____ Harding, U.S. President
10. The _____ of God

Answers

major issues involved. Some issues which other groups have identified are stealing, lying about guilt, legitimate possibility of Robbie arrest, Robbie's attitude toward the whole incident, the role of the pastor, and why the security guard "bluffed" Robbie.

After major issues have been identified, consider the following questions as guides for discussion. Of course, the session should be shaped by the leader, group members, case, and developing flow of the discussion.

● What is Warren Stevens's attitude toward the youth in his church? How would you describe his approach to working with youth at Saluda Baptist Church? Think about his approach.

● How would you describe the pastor (John Pike)? How do you see him as a person? As a youth leader?

● Has Warren planned well for the trip to Six Flags? Enough chaperons? Right types? Other considerations?

● If Robbie Dowd were your friend, how would you answer someone who said: "Tell me about Robbie Dowd." How would you describe him? Why is he your friend?

● How would you explain the money and theft by your friend, Robbie? Was the money his own? Why did he steal the train? Was it for attention? To prove something?

● In addition to what was done, what other *actions could* have been taken about the theft? Lead the group to develop their own list of possibilities. Should you do nothing let Robbie face the legal consequences and be arrested, have Robbie make restitution and apologize, have Warren offer to pay for the train from Robbie's own money, call a meeting of all chaperons to discuss and decide on action, call the youth together to decide, ask the pastor to handle it, send Robbie home alone, or threaten to tell his parents?

Briefly go over the list the group generates, asking what the possible *effect* of each action would be on the persons we know about in the case. If it seems feasible, the group could vote on which they feel is the best action and discuss why. They could "rate" the action possibilities.

Use of (B) Case

An interesting way to use this case is to divide it into two parts, not introducing the second part until completion of discussion of the (A) case. Now introduce the (B) case and give the group a few moments to read what actually happened. Then guide discussion by using the following questions.

● Did Warren do the right thing in paying for the train? Why? What do you think of Robbie's refusal to apologize? Explain.

● Was Warren's arrangement for Robbie to repay later a good one? Could it have been handled in a better way? What about the money in Robbie's wallet? Should there have been some greater immediate penalty for Robbie? If so, what?

● Was it wise not to notify his parents? Should someone have talked with them? Who? What should have been said?

● Do you think Warren did what was best for Robbie? Explain.

● Is there anything else you think Warren might have done to handle this incident better?

Now Let's Get Personal

After the open discussion about Robbie Dowd, consider the personal struggle many persons have with stealing and lying. Consider some of these questions:

● Is stealing (like Robbie did) and cheating in school (stealing a grade) the same thing? How?[15]

● Do you know anyone who has stolen something? What? Is cheating a problem in your school? How? Why?

● When someone steals something, in your experience, does it make a difference if they get caught or not? What is the difference?

Construct a set of agree-disagree statements and ask for group opinions and discussion about each. Here are some examples:

Agree-Disagree?

● Stealing is taking something which does not belong to you. (Does it have to belong to *someone else* in order to be stealing? To whom did the train actually belong?)

- There is never any excuse for stealing. ("Thou shalt not steal" implications?)
- Stealing candy from a store, stealing a bicycle in the neighborhood, and cheating on an exam are the same kind of acts.
- A person who cheats in school will cheat on the job. (Is there a "carryover" of unethical behavior to more than one setting?)
- People who steal must be punished. (What is the role of grace and forgiveness?)
- Honesty is always the best policy. (If so, why have so many of us lied and cheated?)
- Success in business demands some dishonesty and sometimes stealing (stealing of information, personnel, goods, and so forth)

Levels and Questions

Addressing "the more common problems of young people," T. B. Maston identified four levels on which persons can live and make decisions. The *instructive* level is the undisciplined expression of natural desires, hungers, and feelings. The *customary* level is lived by doing what is approved by others, by the mores of the community without regard for whether actions are right or wrong. Thinking through one's values to arrive at reasoned personal moral and ethical guides for living represents the *conscious* level. The *Christian* level for living is characterized by: (1) Christian principles or ideals become the final test for decisions; (2) the Holy Spirit informs and guides one's conscience; (3) the Bible and Holy Spirit are basic to right conduct.[16]

Maston suggests three considerations to guide moral behavior: the effect on us, others, and the cause of Christ. Three tests of right or wrong behavior are; secrecy about it, is it all right for everyone to behave in this manner, and can I invite God to be part of the action?[17]

Introduce Maston's principles and questions and ask the discussants to apply them to the events and persons in this case. For example, one group could work on applying the three aspects of the Christian level and the other group could examine the three suggested tests. All could then discuss the report of the groups.

Juvenile Court counselors Patrick Murphy and Steven Houseworth began "Theft Talk" in Portland, Oregon, in 1980. Their highly successful program involves a one-time, two-hour group discussion about why the youth stole. The basic idea is to underscore that stealing is wrong not because the thief may be caught but because it hurts people financially, emotionally, and sometimes physically. The group could discuss the views of these counselors.

Places of Grace

The youth group is a major source of grace for the Robbie Dowds of the world. Friendship, inclusion, acceptance, caring, and prayer are channels through which God's grace is most likely to reach them. Warren Stevens's leaving this church to return to seminary makes the youth group and adult leaders even more indispensable channels for grace to Robbie.

Do not overlook two words in the crossword puzzle: *love* and *hope*. Though not specifically part of the case, these two doctrines need to be examined. How can love and hope be translated into a language which is understandable to Robbie? To all youth?

Also, do not overlook the potential help which could come from the pastor and his sons. While this source may not be clearly available immediately, these three persons could become a personal spiritual rescue and support team for Robbie. What can Warren Stevens do before he leaves the church to enable such a team to develop?

Assessing Learning

This case leads to reflective thinking which can focus on understanding motives, need for acceptance within the youth group, dilemmas of leading, impact of social class on relationships, and Christian responses to people with problems. Other points of particular importance are: If you have ever stolen anything in the past, what can you say about another who has also stolen? Are we not all beggars looking for a place to get bread? If God has forgiven you, shall you not also forgive another?

Suggested Resources

Elder, Carl. *Youth and Values: Getting Yourself Together*. Nashville: Broadman Press, 1978.

Jeschke, Marlin. *Discipling the Brother: Congregational Discipline According to the Gospel*. Scottsdale, Penn.: Herald Press, 1972.

Is It Right or Wrong? (Equipping Center Module). Nashville: Convention Press, 1984.

3

Youth Camp

"Ted yelled, 'I can't take it anymore,' and ran off into the woods with his knife!" Bobby sputtered excitedly.

Now what? I wonder what it is this time? thought Pastor Ken Gullikson to himself as he heard the news. Ted had done something like this two days ago when he went off into the woods leaving a note behind saying, "I know I am evil and unlovable. I don't think even God can love someone like me. I can't stand it anymore."

Youth Camp[1]

It was Thursday of an annual week-long summer camp for youth of Redeemer Lutheran Church. This particular week focused experiential learning. Each of the five days of activity was organized around a different theme: the Bible, Holy Spirit, church, grace, and world. The topics were studied in the mornings, afternoons were used for recreation, and evenings provided ways for youth to consider their own commitments out of the experiences of the day.

The campsite was nestled in the mountains where the beauty of nature added to the stimulation of the cool, crisp air. Almost without exception, previous participants looked back on the week as an unforgettable experience, even though they might have been initially hesitant about attending. On the whole, Pastor Gullikson felt it had been a positive experience for youth.

Ted Owens

Ted Owens was the youngest of four children. One of his sisters was married, lived away from home, and refused to speak to her father. His other sister was living with her boyfriend. Two years ago Ted's older brother had been placed in a state mental hospital in another part of the state. Both Owens girls were members of Redeemer Lutheran, but only the married sister attended—rarely. The parents had no church membership.

Ted's mother was in favor of religion, but his father openly opposed it. In fact, Mrs. Owens insisted she would gladly have been a regular participant in the church's activities and worship, but to keep peace in the family she stayed home. Home was not peaceful, as often expressed by fights between the parents which sometimes ended with Mrs. Owens locking herself in the bathroom for safety. She had a heart condition and suffered a mild heart attack during the past year. There were many causes for strain in the family, and she claimed she did not care to add religion to the list. Though she did not attend the church, she insisted that Ted attend.

Fortunately there were other church members in the neighborhood with whom Ted could ride to church activities. The pastor could not remember any of Ted's family ever coming to church with him.

A Suspicious Note

Although Ted was intelligent, he was, like many junior high boys, more interested in "goofing off" and girls than in serious Bible study. Part of his motivation to attend camp was the expectation that he might meet some attractive members of the opposite sex. His hopes were not unfounded as he promptly met Stacy Sulivan, a cute blond. He fell in love the first night of camp.

Although Stacy appeared happy with this development, Ted was not and became increasingly depressed with feelings of inferiority, which he expressed to Stacy. Also, he was occasionally verbally abusive to Stacy and, following a disagreement, disappeared one evening leaving a note which hinted at suicide. Stacy and her friends reacted with alarm and quickly went looking for him and brought him back.

Pastor Gullikson had been informed of this situation and had counseled with Ted, convincing him that the best thing to do with his note was to burn it in the campfire. The previous evening each person had written his or her sins on a piece of paper and burned it in the fire, and Gullikson thought this was a good way for Ted to handle this note. Ted quietly tossed the note into the campfire that evening.

How to Help Ted?

Ted was at it again, Ken Gullikson thought. On the surface it appeared that he might be using the same technique which had previously worked so well to get him attention. However, the pastor felt there was more to it than that. That day's study had been on grace. Could Ted's behavior reflect his struggle to accept God's grace?

Pastor Gullikson found himself also wondering if the message of God's grace was getting through to Ted. He went into the woods wondering what he was going to say and do when he found Ted, hopefully without self-inflicted injury.

Ponderings for Pedagogy

Feelings are often mixed in a group when members begin to discuss suicide. Different persons will become uncomfortable, threatened, ashamed, angry, sad, or silent. Yet it is a reality of modern life which has increased in both numbers and pervasiveness. In fact, it is not unusual to discover in many groups person who have to deal with its consequences in their immediate family relatives, friends, or acquaintances. Particularly disturbing and puzzling is the number of older children and youth who have become part of the statistics of suicide. The seriousness of those statistics led Billy Joel to record a music video, "You're Only Human," and designate proceeds from its sale for efforts to prevent youth suicides.

The statistics for the United States fluctuate but remain at levels which are frighteningly high. The following information is from The Suicide Prevention and Education Center, Inc., in Louisville, Kentucky, unless otherwise noted.

• In 1985 suicide was the second leading cause of death among fifteen to twenty-four year olds, fourth among twenty-five to forty-four, eighth among forty-five to sixty-four, and thirteenth for sixty-five and above.

• There is an annual average of 5,000 suicides among youth ages fifteen to twenty-four in the U.S.

• Assuming one out of fifty attempts are successful, some authorities believe there may be 250,000 attempts per year among the fifteen to twenty-four age group, says Dr. Richard Greathouse, Coroner, Jefferson County, Kentucky.

• There is an average of 18,000 adult suicides (ages twenty-five to sixty-four) annually in the U.S.; 5,700 for persons ages sixty-five and above. This means one person commits suicide every 17.8 minutes.

• Males complete suicide three times more often than females.

• Females attempt suicide three times more often than males.

• In 1988 the suicide rate was highest among people older than fifty-five at 20 per 100,000 population, while the national average was 12.1 per 100,000, according to Dr. Greathouse, who believes suicides in this age group are 15-29 percent underreported. His reasons were: (1) Death appears to be from natural causes, and (2) Pressures not to report it as suicide.

• Nevada leads the country in suicides. Their rate is 29 per 1,000 for fifteen to twenty-four-year-old residents while the national rate is 13 per 1,000 for that age group.

The causes of teenage suicide continue to be studied, but a "conscious, deliberate attempt to take one's life quickly"[2] has been part of cultures from the Greeks onward. Indeed, Gerald Adams and Thomas Gullotta note that some early Christians, seeing earthly existence as unimportant and life as being filled with temptations to sin, committed suicide in order to gain immediate entrance into an eternal life of complete happiness.[3] Alvarey contends in *The Savage God* that it was not until Augustine's writings against suicide that the Council of Orleans in A.D. 533 ruled it a sin.[4]

Simple or single factor theories explaining suicide have been widely questioned and often disproved. Theories which seek to explain adolescent suicide may be grouped, however, into psychoanalytic and sociological perspectives. *Psychoanalytic* explanations center on internal variables such as punishment of others, sexual issues, and feelings of hopelessness and suggest there may also be suicidal personalities. *Sociological* approaches point to external forces: anomie (lack of purpose, identity, rootlessness) within the family, emotional deprivation, the value of religious cultures as deterrents, and so forth.[5]

Dr. Greathouse speaks out of experience with youth suicides in suggesting three important causal possibilities. The first is *affluence* which makes drugs and alcohol easy to purchase. "Almost half of all our suicides are chemically related to drugs," he reports. Second, teenagers are *impulsive,* reaching quickly to sudden changes in their lives without thinking about consequences. Third, and to him the most important, "kids used to have a clear idea about *rules, and regulations, and responsibilities.* These have eroded over the last two decades. They don't know what to expect or what is expected of them."[6]

The quality of relationships within both nuclear and extended family units was identified as a primary cause of suicide in a 1987 Burns Roper survey of eight to seventeen-year-old boys and girls which was conducted for the American Chicle Group. Ninety percent were generally happy with their home life, and 93 percent reported satisfaction with the amount of love received from parents. However, only sixty-two respondents were happy about relationships with siblings. Only 79 percent were satisfied with the amount of time parents spent with them. What would improve home life? Thirty percent said more open conversation with parents, being treated as adults, more time with parents, having more money, being given more responsibility, and parents getting along better.[7]

One form of adolescent suicide presents a special challenge to family members and the experts who seek to explain it. *Cluster suicide* was tragically illustrated in March 1987 when four teenagers locked themselves in a garage in Bergenfield, New Jersey, wrote a suicide note, started the car, and died of carbon monoxide poisoning. This shocking event was seen by many as being linked to four other teenage suicides during the previous eight months in Bergenfield. It was identified as a "copycat suicide." Common factors included school difficulties (which sometimes had led to expulsion or dropping out), reticence to approach officials for help, alienation, drugs and alcohol, and a feeling there was an absence of consistent parental support.[8]

The next day, in Alsip, Illinois, two teenagers, ages nineteen and seventeen, best friends, neighbors, and classmates, killed themselves by the same method. Both were school dropouts and left notes, nine in all, to friends and relatives. Seven notes were on the dashboard and two under the windshield wiper. Authorities doubted (but were not certain) that these suicides were connected to the four in New Jersey. A failed marriage, lack of school success, and feelings of having disappointed their parents were reported.[9]

One of every ten youth in America is at risk of committing suicide. Ted Owens is one of those youth. His life presents a variety of factors which are often included in the lists of causes of suicide.

Group Leadership

Dramatis Personae

Attention should be given first to the persons involved: Pastor Gullikson, Ted, Mrs. Owens, and Stacy. Invite discussants to suggest words or concepts which characterize each one. For example, Gullikson may be seen as a conscientious, sensitive, hardworking, counselor, teacher, or man of God. It may be helpful to ask about the way in which Ted views himself (inferior, pressured, unaccepted, and so forth). Here are some possibilities suggested by others who have discussed the case.

Pastor Gullikson	Ted Owens	Stacy Sullivan	Mother
conscientious	intelligent	blond	supportive
sensitive	youngest	cute	heart trouble
counselor	family pressures	forceful	peacemaker
teacher	inferiority	games	caring
concerned	troubled		
diligent	atypical		

What sort of feelings do you have for or about each of these? Admiration, anger, suspicion, trust . . . what? (Let group respond).

Look at Ted and Stacy's relationship. What observations would you make about it? How did it come to be? Why did it develop? Exactly what *is* Ted's relationship to Stacy? How do you describe it? Does Ted feel inferior to Stacy? Why? Does the fact that she is from a stable family and seems confident of herself bother Ted? Is she domineering? What role does the relationship give or create for Ted? Does he like it? What kind of influence do you see from Ted's family on how he is relating to Stacy? Are there parallels between his home experience and the way in which he relates to Stacy?

Issues/Themes

This case highlights one youth, like so many others, who feels overwhelmed by the *pressures and complexities* of his existence. Youth like Ted feel lonely and hopeless, and they view life only in terms of the present. In their desperation they may consider suicide as a certain and complete solution to their problem.

The dramatic threat of suicide should be seen in its relationship to several other themes. Ted's *home* is one of conflict and tension and is unlikely to encourage his stability and happiness. Mrs. Owens's health and the institutional commitment of Ted's brother contribute the theme of *illness* and its impact on others. Ted also seems to be struggling with a low *self-image* which may produce feelings of inferiority and a desire for escape. The role of the *pastor* and *church* in Ted's life are significant factors which also deserve consideration.

Help group members identify what they see as specific issues in the case. Some groups have examined evidences of both theological and human issues, without attempting to separate these two categories. This approach resulted in the following ideas.

Love.—Is he responding to the way he has seen his family model love? Hiding versus confrontation? Affection at home? Father's love? Can he accept God's love?

Grace.—Extension through pastor? Are others mediating grace to Ted? What are some other ways God's grace could be channeled to him? Is Ted finding acceptance of unmerited, unearned love difficult?

Burning note.—Good idea? Why? Is it a superficial way to deal with real, known, and acknowledged sin?

Feelings of inferiority.—In his mind, how might Ted feel his home compares to those of other youth? Would you agree with James Dobson's statement: "An 'epidemic of inferiority' still rages among the young (and haunts the mature)?"[10]

Forgiveness.—How does the forgiveness of God fit into the circumstances in Ted's home? What does he understand by it? Can he forgive himself for his actions and the situation?

Modeling.—The modeling of home life, parents, siblings, and personal difficulty contribute to Ted's feelings. In what ways are his coping responses to life like those of his mother (hiding, searching for peace, or illness)? His father's?

Possible Actions for Pastor Gullikson

What immediate actions are open to Gullikson, assuming Ted has not harmed himself as yet?

Find him.—Then get the knife away from Ted. What can he do or say to get the knife from Ted?

Reinforce his caring for Ted.—After retrieving the knife (if he can), what should Gullikson's response be to the threat? If Gullikson decides to go after Ted, what should he be prepared to say? Do? What "message" or strategy should underlie what he says and does? How can he reinforce his caring for Ted? "We all care. I came, didn't I? Remember that other youth came after you on Tuesday, didn't they? We are here for you." Remind him of the pastor's visit and desire for Ted to be at the camp. Express care by Ted's mother and her desire for him to be there and have a happy, safe experience.

Talk.—Get him to talk. Assure him: "We can work things out." This is an opportunity to have two persons role play the conversation between Ted and Gullikson. Select these persons in advance and do not select people who are depressed, in the midst of family turmoil, or show signs of thinking about suicide. Also, do not let the actors give arguments *for* suicide without challenging those arguments.

Ted may need continued help at a level of expertise which Pastor Gullikson is neither equipped nor able to provide. If he feels it is needed, how should Gullikson attempt referral?

What Can We Learn about Suicide?

Group members should be encouraged to examine three important things they need to know about suicide.

• What are some *signs* that a person may be contemplating suicide?

• What can *I do* to help prevent suicide in another person?

• Where and how can *help be secured* for a suicidal person?

Mistaken ideas.—Because there are so many myths about suicide, it is wise to lead persons to examine and correct any misinformation they possess. An interesting way to do this is by use of *true-false* statements. Those which follow have been gleaned from many sources and used with a number of groups.

• If he talks about it, he won't do it. (One study reported 85 percent who talked about it and committed suicide).

• She tried it before. She won't do it again. (Up to 80 percent had tried it before.)

• Talking about it to youth will tempt them to commit suicide. (On the contrary, evidence suggests just the opposite.)

- Most suicide victims will leave a note or message to survivors. (Few actually do.)
- If someone is going to kill himself, he will not give clues. (Clues may be intended but are often missed because they are "coded" by the person.)
- Girls are more likely to attempt suicide than boys. (Girls attempt suicide three times more often than boys. Attempts by boys are three times more likely to be successful and are done by more violent means.)
- High achievers in high school rarely consider their own suicide. (*Who's Who Among American High School Students* reported in 1988 that 31 percent said they had considered it.)
- Most suicidal people do not want to die and want to be discovered and stopped. (They want the pain, trouble, and problems in their lives to go away and do not know how to help themselves.)
- Adolescent suicide occurs most often in summer and winter months. (April, May, and August are most common with youth.)
- Even hospital clinicians tend to deny, minimize, or not to recognize suicidal clues.
- A potentially suicidal youth and her/his family should be cautious about getting involved too quickly in a treatment program because of the stigma it may create for the youth.

Answers: F, F, T, F, F, F, T, F, T, F, T, F.

Clues

Experts have studied presuicide behavior of youth in an effort to isolate signs, acts, and clues which can identify a person who needs help.

- Making changes in behavior. Though they do not always signal an impending suicide, any *abrupt changes* in school performance, interests, and "favorite" activities need to be observed and evaluated. Self-destructive risk-taking (alcohol, running away, drugs, reckless driving, vandalizing); withdrawn behavior, eating and sleep disturbances, and apathy toward everything (ennui) can also indicate the possibility of suicide.
- Giving away prized possessions may be preparation for suicide. An eleven-year-old girl gave her pencil case to a friend on the school bus before going home and killing herself. Be alert to statements like: "I may not be here next year." "If I ever said anything to hurt you, I'm sorry." "I won't need this. I want you to have it."
- Setting unrealistic goals which guarantee failure, which becomes the reason to "end it all."

- Breaking up a serious boy-girl relationship. Other disappointments such as not making the team and family separation or divorce are times when special attention and support are needed.
- Having trauma from injury or illness, pregnancy, abortion, unhappiness over change of residence, firing, and so forth.
- Talking about it. "I think I'll just kill myself." "How do you kill yourself?" "Everyone would be better off without me around." "Nobody would miss me if I were dead."
- Producing artwork or writing about death.
- Accumulating the means for suicide: the weapon, drugs, rope, poison, cleaning fluids, detergents, antihistamines, amphetamines, and so forth. Examine the strength or power of the means on a lethality scale.
- Experiencing death of a family member, friend, well-liked teacher, or idol, especially if it is a known suicide or by violent means. Sixty-five percent of teenage suicides had knowledge of the suicide of someone else. Feeling "I can do it, too," or "It won't hurt them to be without me" appear to be factors.
- Being a victim of physical or sexual abuse. In addition to abuse from other sources, there is also an alarming rise in abuse within dating or boyfriend/girlfriend relationships.
- Verbalizing thoughts about suicide. Examples: "I wish I weren't around," "Just keep on and you'll be sorry," "I hope I sleep forever and don't get up again," "I don't care. There won't be a tomorrow," "Soon I'll be out of the way," "I guarantee soon you won't have me around to bully and pick on."
- Seeing destructive and impulsive behavior, including fire-setting; antisocial behavior; or cruelty to siblings, peers, or animals.
- Being a "do nothing."
- Telling a peer or "near peer" of his or her intentions.

Intervention Strategies

Friends and relatives who care will desire to prevent suicide but may find it difficult to decide how to help. While keeping in mind that there is never assurance of successfully preventing a determined person from committing suicide, what are some guidelines for trying?

- Watch what they are *doing* to "act out" their intentions. Are there expressions or signs which give clues or raise suspicions?
- Communicate that you hear and are receiving their clues. Ask questions, remembering that questions never "give" the idea of suicide to someone else. Examples: "Are you thinking of killing yourself?" "When people feel bad, they sometimes hurt themselves. Are you thinking of hurting yourself?" If so, "How do you plan to do it?"

"Do you have the means already?" "Where will you do it? When?" (Some data suggest teenage suicides occur most often between 3:00 p.m. and midnight.)

● If there is evidence or suspicion of an imminent attempt, do not leave the person alone. Acknowledge the possibility of suicide with the person but help him/her to examine other alternative solutions to life's problems. "Have you considered this possibility?"

● Never be judgmental about beliefs or behavior. Never communicate that "God is going to get you for this." Do not argue or "debate" with the person, since this could increase feelings of alienation and despair.

● Don't be helpless or hopeless with the person.

● Wayne E. Oates, a recognized authority in counseling, made the following suggestions to several classes in youth ministry. (1) Notify your pastor. (2) Mobilize support persons. Who art the most important persons to him or her? Sunday School teacher? Family friend? School teacher? Have that person intervene. (3) Establish contact with the family, especially if a young person is involved. (4) If you have done all you can, seek help from the person's doctor or have parents consult the doctor. (5) Maintain the lines of communication and project future actions to be taken by the person such as set a time when you will see him or her again. "When you feel this way again, pick up the phone and call me. Come to see me or tell me where you are, and I will come to you." "Write to me." "Promise me you won't do it. Get in touch with me first."

● Contact professional help if you think it is serious. Do not delay or take a risk with another person's life.

● Be informed about the problem ahead of time. Help others to be informed through discussion, books, speakers, seminars, parent-youth-worker trialogues, and so forth.

Biblical Material

Bill Blackburn, counselor, pastor, and author, points out that there are six cases of suicide in the Bible. They are:

● Abimelech (Judg. 9:50-55)
● Samson (Judg. 16:23-31)
● Saul (1 Sam. 31:1-6; 2 Sam. 1:1-27; 1 Chron. 10:1-14)
● Ahithophel (2 Sam. 17:23)
● Zimri (1 Kings 16:15-20)
● Judas (Matt. 27:5)

Blackburn notes those cases are reported with little comment. Second, the Bible does not directly condemn suicide. Third, "the clear teaching of Scripture is that suicide is wrong. Life is a gift from God and is to be used responsibly and redemptively."[11] It should be added that suicide is not identified as the unpardonable sin. The unpardonable sin is resistance to the work of the Holy Spirit which leads to salvation. The unpardonable sin is the continual refusal of God's gift of salvation.

Oates says that God expects us to make our own decisions except about when we will die. Only God makes that decision, and only He can assign sin and condemnation to our choices in life. God alone can define "unpardonable sin," and there is no biblical evidence defining it as suicide.

Suggested Resources

• Contact the Suicide Prevention and Education Center or its equivalent for resources, speakers, and seminars.

• Contact the Suicide Hotline, Rape Relief Center, Child Abuse Hotline, Safe Place (Runaway), Al-Anon-Ala-Teen, Drug Education/Abuse Center, or other appropriate local resource center.

• Check the public library for books, magazines, and other media on suicide. The following are some books to consider.

Kubler-Ross, Elizabeth. *Remember the Secret.* Millbrae, Calif.: Celestial Arts, 1982. (Ages child-adult).

Blackburn, Bill. *What You Should Know About Suicide.* Waco, Tx.: Word Books, 1982. (Excellent theology and practical ideas for helping).

Frandsen, Kathryn J., and Hafen, Brent Q. *Youth Suicide: Depression and Loneliness.* Provo, Utah: Behavioral Health Associates, 1986.

Joan, Polly. *Preventing Teenage Suicide: The Living Alternative Book.* New York: Human Sciences Press, 1986.

Hewett, John H. *After Suicide.* Philadelphia: The Westminster Press, 1980.

Ross, Richards and Hayes, Judi, comps. *Ministry to Youth in Crisis.* Nashville: Convention Press, 1988. (See chapter 3, "Ministry in a Suicidal Crisis" by Bill Blackburn.)

Rowatt, G. Wade, Jr. *Pastoral Care with Adolescents in Crisis.* Louisville, Ky.: Westminster/John Knox Press, 1989. (See chapter 8, "Depression and Suicide.")

4

Tragedy on a Retreat

When the seminary professor said a summer internship as a youth minister would "be good experience," he *certainly didn't have this in mind*, thought Bill Hayes. As he drove into the church parking lot with his three subdued teenage passengers, he shook his head as if to clear his mind and grasp what had happened. The experiences of the past eight hours were shocking. Yet, he felt most frightened by the prospect of talking with Jessie Thomas's parents. *What am I going to say to them? How can I explain the accident?* Bill thought. How he wished for a pastor who could go with him (or *for* him) to see Mr. and Mrs. Thomas.

Summer Retreat (A)

At the end of his first year in seminary, Bill Hayes decided to earn field education credit by working in a church as summer youth minister. His faculty adviser suggested San Carlos Baptist Church, which had requested such a minister, and said he would like to recommend Bill. Bill agreed, was interviewed by the church, and was employed.

The church was located in a small California town. Church membership was approximately 500, with about 250 active participants. Finances were adequate for existing and projected needs. The church was without a regular pastor. (The previous one left after experiencing considerable tension with the congregation.) Dr. John Tisdale, the interim preacher, was a retired minister who lived fifty miles away. Tisdale drove to the San Carlos church on Sunday morning and returned home after evening services.

Retreat Planning

The youth retreat was to be the climax of the summer youth program. When Bill arrived at the church, the general location for the retreat had been determined. He was expected to plan the details, program, and so forth. This he did with considerable input from youth and adult leaders. It was a tent-camping retreat in a national park (an hour and a half drive) which bordered on the Pacific Ocean and provided long hiking trails. Conversation with park rangers revealed a minor danger of snakes and a major danger from the white cliffs which over-looked part of the beach and could produce unexpected landslides.

Youth and counselors agreed to a Wednesday through Friday pro-gram the last week in July. On the appointed day, twenty-five youth and five counselors joined Bill in arriving at the retreat site at 9:00 a.m. Tents were erected on the platforms provided and a brief devotional preceded some free time before lunch. Hiking, swimming, viewing the cliffs, Bible study, and discussion sessions filled the remainder of Wednesday and Thursday. Bill felt that Thursday evening was particu-larly effective with its periods of Bible study, personal prayer, prayer partners, and campfire service. "The kids are on a real spiritual high," he told Lucy Armstrong, one of the counselors.

Thursday evening Bill became concerned about the illness of Jessie Thomas. In fact, he tried to persuade Jessie to return home with an older teenager who was driving back to town because of work the next day. Jessie insisted he would "feel OK later" and wanted to stay. After talking with Jessie's uncle, counselor Marvin Peterson, Bill reluctantly agreed for him to stay. Jessie remained on his cot in his tent and seemed all right the next morning.

The Friday Morning Tragedy

Following a leisurely breakfast on Friday, the group gathered at the cliff area for 10:00 a.m. Bible study. At 10:30 the youth were told there was free time until lunch at 12:30 p.m., which would be followed by a closing session and packing for the return trip.

Accompanied by counselors Marvin and Marge Peterson, Bill re-turned to the campsite to help another counselor prepare for lunch, leaving two counselors with the youth.

About forty-five minutes after arriving at the campsite, Bill and the Petersons were alarmed by the sound of sirens on the nearby road, a sound which seemed to be moving in the direction of the cliffs. They decided to take their truck to a close-by entrance to the trail and hike to the cliff area. On the trail they were surprised to meet Jim Thomas who seemed on the verge of tears. To their questions, he replied, "Haven't you heard? Jessie's been hurt." Bill quickly urged Jim to re-turn to their retreat campsite while he and the Petersons hurried to the cliff area. On their arrival, Lucy Armstrong reported in a low whisper, "Jessie is dead. The rangers are here and have taken over." A body lay nearby covered by a blanket.

The Cliffs

Lucy explained that while some youth swam or beachcombed, five boys had climbed the short slope under the edge of the highest cliff in order to "leave something from the retreat." They intended to scratch a "one-way sign" and cross in the clay on the cliff's wall. Suddenly a youth watching from below shouted "Avalanche!" The other youth managed to get away but Jessie, seeking to outrun the slide, was overtaken and struck by the clay and rocks.

Jessie's brother, Jim , had witnessed the accident and appeared to be in a state of shock. Recognizing this, Lucy tried to console him (he did not realize his brother was dying) and sent him back to find Bill, whom he met on the trail. She reported, "After a few minutes of difficult breathing, I thought there was no pulse in Jessie's body, but I didn't want to tell Jim that."

Responding to Tragedy

The rangers stationed nearby had arrived on the scene quickly and assumed control of the situation. They confirmed to Lucy Armstrong that Jessie was dead and indicated the body could not be moved until the local authorities had arrived and determined the exact circumstances of Jessie's death. Further, they instructed the group to remain until the sheriff arrived since witnesses to the accident would need to be available to give him their statements, if they were required.

Following the sheriff's questioning and arranging for the body to be sent home, the youth group returned to the campsite. After talking with the other leaders, Bill decided to have a brief time of prayer and let the youth cry for awhile. About fifteen to twenty minutes later he decided to concentrate on keeping them busy in preparation for leaving. During this time Marvin Peterson reported privately to Bill that Jim had said, "It's the Lord's will. The Lord has a plan for this, I'm sure."

Bill commented: "I guess that's the way he feels right now. It is good that he is able to be spiritual about it right now."

Bill and the Petersons agreed it would be unwise to call Jessie's parents by telephone. Instead, Marvin Peterson said that his brother, Tony Peterson, who was a minister, was in their town visiting and could be asked to inform Al and Gladys Thomas of the tragedy. Tony knew them well. This request was made by phone, and Tony agreed to make the visit. Also, a message was left on Dr. Tisdale's telephone answering machine.

Leaving the camp area at about 4:15 p.m., the group arrived at church before 6:00 p.m.

Dealing with the Crisis

After some discussion, Bill and the Petersons prepared to take Jim home. Tony Peterson drove into the parking lot and advised against it. He reported that Al Thomas was furious, not at anyone in particular. It was agreed it would be best for Tony to take Jim home and Bill to call on the Thomases later.

That evening Al Thomas called Marvin Peterson saying he wanted to meet with Lucy Armstrong, the Petersons, and Bill at 10:00 p.m. at his home. He indicated that Jim seemed unable to talk about the incident, had been given a tranquilizer, and was put to bed.

The meeting revolved around Lucy's efforts to explain that there was no misbehaving, the youth were not in a forbidden area, and it truly was an accident. Gladys Thomas commented: "We know Jessie was a Christian. It's God's will, and we will have to work through it." Bill felt she was being tremendous and spiritual about the whole thing. However, Al was very accusative, and as the meeting was ending, he was cursing, demanding to see the campsite, and threatening to sue somebody. As Bill and the Petersons walked to their cars, Bill reassured them that these were normal reactions.

On Saturday Bill visited Jessie's grandparents, whom he had come to know fairly well. The grandfather said little. However, in spite of Bill's efforts to clarify and explain the accident, the grandmother was direct: "I think it was the fault of your workers and the church. It is impossible for five adults to watch after twenty-five teenagers. You are responsible for what happened. You should have had enough adults so you could be with them all the time."

Saturday afternoon Bill also spent time at the Petersons' home with Marvin, Marge, and Lucy as they tried to deal with their own shock and questions. They felt "somehow responsible" and repeatedly asked why. Lucy remarked: "Every time I close my eyes I see Jessie taking his last breath and hear that gurgling sound his breathing made."

They all anticipated with mixed emotions the next day's youth Sunday School classes and worship services.

Summer Retreat (B)

Note: Both A and B cases may be read by the group before any group discussion. Another method is to read A first, followed by discussion, then introduce B and follow it with further discussion. "Group Leadership" suggestions include these options.

At Bill's suggestion, the four youth Sunday School classes were combined for their Sunday morning Bible study. Lucy's husband (who was the department director) tried to conduct a brief program but quickly broke into tears. Youth were crying "on and off" as Bill arose to take over and attempt to deal briefly with Psalm 23.

In the morning worship service, the youth sat together, and, during the time of commitment at the end of the service, twenty to twenty-five came forward, some weeping. Dr. Tisdale later explained to Bill that he thought this very appropriate. He added, "These youth experienced a tragedy. They know death is real and that the end of life brings either heaven or hell. Their responses were valid and desirable."

The Funeral

The funeral service was crowded on Monday morning. Dr. Tisdale and Reverend Ted Sneed, who had baptized Jessie some years earlier, conducted the service. Bill Hayes delivered a eulogy and read a "Letter to God" which Jessie, like all youth on the retreat, had written as part of the Thursday evening campfire program.

At the conclusion of the service, Dr. Tisdale issued an invitation for commitment, suggesting such decisions could be indicated by standing. The crowd was astonished to see Al and then Gladys Thomas stand and then to be followed by Jessie's grandmother and grandfather. The people wept and rejoiced simultaneously, since Gladys was the only professed Christian and church member.

Steve Perry's Guilt

Bill had learned on Sunday evening that Steve Perry had some deep-seated feelings of guilt about the accident. Being one of the youth to escape, Steve was present at and immediately following the slide. Bill called Steve and invited him to lunch on Tuesday. The invitation was accepted.

Trying to explain his feelings, Steve indicated he was an Eagle Scout and had received first aid training which included mouth-to-mouth resuscitation. "When I was faced with a real situation I just couldn't do it. I just couldn't do it. I didn't even try. It might have saved Jessie's life," he told me.

Bill responded, "I, too, feel somewhat guilty about it, Steve. I think of what might have been if I had only sent him home Thursday night. I feel I had a responsibility in the whole affair, but I am not responsible for the accident. It *was* an accident. You simply must accept the fact this is the Lord's will. The Lord has a plan for this."

Reflecting on the Experience

With a cup of coffee in hand, Bill Hayes tried to relax on Tuesday evening and began to think about the whole experience. *What should be done next? How can I evaluate the retreat and its associated events? Conclusions about the whole thing*? In the back of his mind he knew he would also have to answer questions like these when he reported on his summer's work to his faculty supervisor in four weeks.

Ponderings for Pedagogy

The French philosopher La Rochefoucauld once wrote that "Death is like the sun; no one can look at it directly. . . . But if I never look at death even indirectly, then death will always take me by surprise."[1] Yet American society discourages our looking. For example, actor-producer Michael Landon reported that NBC sought to persuade him to delete the word *die* from his film "Where Pigeons Go to Die." Landon refused, saying that "I think they liked something stunning like 'Welcome Home, Grandfather.' "[2]

Whether it results from accident, suicide, or disease the death of a child or youth is sad and traumatic for those who remain. The younger the victim the more tragic the sense of loss is. Pertinent to this case is the fact that the largest number of deaths among American youth is classified as "accidental," making it the leading killer of young people.

Themes

The accidental death of a teenager on a church-sponsored retreat is the obvious theme in this case. A related theme is how to *help youth cope* with the reality that all of us will die. Youth often do not like to think about death because they want to feel that death is for others. They choose to live out the illusion that it will not happen to them.

Theological themes are likely to surface. They may address the reasons for human existence and the relation to our lives of the God who created us. Why does a God who loves us let us become victims of such tragedies? If God is all-powerful and wishes to overcome evil with good, why does He not intervene in our behalf and prevent them?

Perceptions about the nature of the *will of God* are strongly evident in the statements of several persons in the case, including those of Bill Hayes. There is the clear assignment to God's will of the accident which caused Jessie Thomas's death. Is this a way for us to cope with our own shock, or does God in fact allow such tragedies in order to "accomplish His will" or teach us certain lessons, painful though they be? How does this relate to the more fundamental question of the *nature of God?*

Uses

This case is well suited to many purposes. Some leaders have found it helpful in guiding youth through their grief over the loss of a member of their youth group, a relative, or a friend. It raises important questions about the function of grief in the midst of loss, of whatever kind (divorce, moving, death of a pet). To the surprise of some, youth have shown that death is a matter which they have considerable interest, when the subject is handled responsibly. Perhaps this is due at least partly to their concern about what happens after death, which Merton Strommen reported finding in his research.[3] In an effort to deal constructively with this subject, one youth leader planned several sessions in which youth were led to examine views about death held by several major religions and climaxed the studies with a visit to a funeral home where the entire process of burial preparation was sensitively explained and discussed.

Situations in this case are useful to include in youth retreats, workshops, and training sessions designed to prepare adult leaders to help youth cope with tragedy in their lives. It is also an excellent vehicle for developing peer counseling skills and support *before* tragedy comes.

During and Following the Immediate Crisis

Two periods of adjustment which follow loss due to death are dealing with the immediate trauma and the long-term adjustment to the permanent loss. Drawing from many sources, this section provides suggestions and ideas for dealing with both phases.

Having experienced the loss of his college-age daughter in an automobile accident and having led several youth groups in their coping with tragic loss, Wade Rowatt, professor of psychology of religion, offers a number of suggestions for helping survivors cope with loss.

First, recognize that grief is a natural reaction to loss or trauma in life experience. You cannot keep youth from hurting, but you may help them cope and, hopefully, grow beyond the experience. Several stages may occur in the grief process, though not all will appear, and those that do will not be in a clearly precise order for each grieving person.

Shock—Grief starts the moment we learn of death, even if we know it is coming. Numbness. It may last few minutes to years.

Flood of emotion or pain—May be expressed in many ways such as crying, laughing, silence, hysteria, and so forth. Encourage ventilation of feelings. Be still and let God love them through you. Offer a shoulder to cry on. People don't necessarily need words; they need presence.

Emotions—May be expressed in at least three forms:
   • *Depression.* May not eat, just sleep. Help them get over and through it. Don't let them pull back: "You can get beyond this suffering if you will to do so."

- *Anger.* May be in all directions, including toward you and God. "It's OK to be angry but focus it appropriately."
- *Guilt.* Two types are "real" guilt and "what if" guilt.

Physical reactions—Ulcers, asthma, arthritis, and so forth may result. A person may give up, turn to alcohol or drugs, or even die.

Fantasy versus reality—Won't let go, keeps ring, picture, clothes or maintains room same as before death.

Acceptance—Recognize that pain is necessary to come to this stage. Achieve assurance that we "grieve not as those who have no hope."

Rowatt also suggests the value of having youth present to talk and help work through it. A carefully planned funeral ritual with appropriate tone and content is positive and hope-filled; while acknowledging grief. Recognize the potential for spiritual change and growth which exists even in the midst of their grief.[4]

Earl Grollman has worked with bereaved children and is the author of *Explaining Death to Children.* He lists feelings associated with grief: shock and denial, physical problems, anger, guilt, and a range of other reactions such as trying to assume the place/role of a parent, attempting to walk or talk like the deceased person, and exaggerating good qualities of the dead person.[5]

Harold Kushner prods us to think carefully before crediting God with causing or having some hidden reason for bringing or allowing tragedies to afflict us. Some people would explain tragedy as God's way to teach us a lesson (the nature of which we do not know), to get us to change our lives or behavior, get our attention, test us as He did Abraham (Gen. 22:1-18) or Job, or "liberate us from a world of pain and lead us to a better place." Citing Psalm 121:1-2, Kushner suggests that God does not cause bad things to happen to us nor does He take pleasure in our tragedies. Instead, when bad things happen to us, He is our source of help for coping with them. They are not automatically to be interpreted as "God's will."[6]

Surviving loved ones need even more support and help after the funeral. Chaplain William Justice reports some disturbing data about post-funeral calling by ministers. One study by Charles Backmann found that few grieving people are visited "once they walk away from the grave." Another three-year mini-study by Gay Harris, regional chaplain for a chain of seven funeral homes, found similar neglect. Justice says of Harris's study that without exception those who used the services of a "borrowed pastor" for a funeral never again had a contact from either the pastor or the church he represented.

Further, of the sixty percent in Harris's study who were church members, only 25 percent received one pastoral visit after the day of the funeral. No one received a second visit. Thus, 75 percent of the church members did not receive *one* follow-up call, while the other 25 percent received only one. Only 15 percent of all persons in Harris's study received one pastoral visit following the funeral of their loved one.[7]

Three excellent sources of ideas for helping persons after the funeral are as follows:

> William Justice, *When Death Comes* (Nashville: Broadman Press, 1982), chapter 5.
> Blackburn, Bill, and Blackburn, Deana Mattingly, *Caring in Times of Family Crisis* (Nashville: Convention Press, 1987), chapters 5 and 6.
> Grisham, Jack, *Helping Persons Who Grieve,* (Women's Missionary Union: Birmingham, Ala., n.d.), especially 71-81.

Joe Baroody, director of pastoral care, McLeod Regional Medical Center, Florence, South Carolina, proposes that death has four aspects: *thing* of death (its personal character), *sting* of death (connection with sin), *ring* of death (fear), and promise we can *sing* in spite of it (connection with new life).[8] To deal with the death of a youth, Baroody uses the Beatitude, "Blessed are they that mourn: for they shall be comforted" (Matt. 5:4) and suggests six beatitudes which can help survivors to move away from despair and toward hope.[9]

1. Be rather than flee.
2. Allow their pain rather than explain.
3. Hold rather than scold.
4. Give hugs not drugs.
5. Empathize rather than sympathize. To empathize is the effort to see things as others do, feel as they feel, and communicate that understanding back to them.
6. The reality of the finality. Helping them achieve acceptance and closure.

Group Leadership

Consider beginning the discussion with the following list of stress levels represented by the life events listed. List on a chalkboard, newsprint, or overhead transparency and ask group members to rate from the most to the least stressful.[10]

1. Pregnancy
2. Death of a spouse
3. Son or daughter leaving home
4. Divorce
5. Change in residence
6. Personal injury or illness
7. Death of a close friend

8. Trouble with in-laws
9. Fired at work
10. Jail term
11. Marital separation
12. Change in church activities
(Correct order as reported by Dr. Keith Sehnert is as follows: 2,4,11,10,6,9,1,7,3,8,5,12.)

Discuss the loss of a child and how stressful group members feel it would be in comparison to the other items. Guide them to examine the case study.

Another way to begin is to list the following words on a chalkboard: *parent, spouse, child, friend*. Point out that these four human losses deeply affect all of us. "Regardless of how strong or comforting religious beliefs may be, death means the loss of a living being, the absence of a physical presence. It is a time of sadness and mourning."[11] It creates overwhelming feelings of tragedy and sets in motion some form of grief process.

Elizabeth Kubler-Ross's stages of denial or isolation, anger, bargaining, depression, and acceptance-hope may be introduced and briefly discussed. It is wise, however, to remember that Kubler-Ross's stages were posited for terminally ill patients.[12] Further, UCLA Professor Edwin Schneidman and others have challenged her stages, holding that rather than passing through stages, "if you stand up well to life, you'll do all right in death."[13]

A question which may be asked at this point could also be chosen as another way to begin the group session. Ask: Have you been present when someone died? Natural causes? Through an accident?' If so, ask about the witness' feelings. How did you cope with it?

Suggest that there are many ways in which people cope with a tragic loss. List some ways of coping on the chalkboard and ask the group to identify the persons in this case who illustrate each response. Here is a list, along with some persons who appear to be responding in that way to Jessie's death: *Shock*—Jim Thomas; *Denial*—Jim Thomas; *Calm*—Marvin and Marge Peterson; *Guilt*—Bill, Marvin and Marge Peterson; *Blame*—Grandparents; *Explanations of accidents as God's will*—Jim Thomas, Gladys Thomas, Bill Hayes; *Explanations of accidents as accidents*—Lucy.

Another technique for looking at these coping strategies is to list the names and then ask, What is each of these persons saying (words) about the tragedy? Lead the group to consider ways in which each person is demonstrating his or her efforts to cope through actions, specific statements, or feeling levels. Note that persons may use more than one of these coping behaviors.

In this story, Bill Hayes has to cope with the tragedy in several ways. Guide the discussion to include his guilt feelings, efforts to explain the tragedy as God's will, talking with others (parents, grandparents, Marvin, Marge, Lucy), and his feeling of helplessness.

Lead the group to identify and examine some of the issues which they see arising from the (A) part of the case. Examples of issues suggested by other groups are:

● Responsibility of the minister of youth and church for accidents involving church groups.

● Could this tragedy have been prevented? Why? How?

● Interpretation of the accident as "the will of God." How best should it be understood?

● Did Bill Hayes handle the whole incident properly? In what way?

Some groups have found this case can be effectively studied if it is separated into two parts, the separation being at the point of anticipating "Youth Sunday School classes and worship services." Discussion has first included only the (A) case and the procedures listed earlier. If this choice is made, deal next with all the possible *action options* which Bill Hayes and others have open to them in the (A) case. Examine the possible effects of each action. The group could even decide what they think is the *best action* for him to take. Then introduce the (B) case and allow time for the discussants to read it.

Now guide the discussion based on the total case. Consider these questions for aiding participation.

1. What was Dr. Tisdale's assessment of the morning worship experience? What do you feel about his assessment?
2. How do you feel about Dr. Tisdale's giving an invitation at the funeral? Is this manipulating people?
3. Was Bill helpful to Steve Perry? Was he wise to share his own guilt feelings? What is Bill's concept of "the Lord's will"? What do you think he means by "a plan for this"?
4. What has this experience done for Bill Hayes? How has it affected him? What do you feel he has learned? Has it made him a better minister? How?
5. Can you identify some things we can learn from this experience? What are some remaining needs or problems which will need attention from the church staff, particularly Bill Hayes, and the church congregation?

It will be helpful to consider at this point the "resources of grace" perceived by the group. List and discuss their suggestions. Possibilities: Tony Peterson, Dr. Tisdale, prayer, caring congregation, trust in Bill Hayes.

Finding Help in the Bible

Strommen found that the youth in his research who professed "consensual" or "intrinsic" religious faith were divided as to whether "If I say I believe in God and do right, I will go to heaven." Fifty-three percent said yes and 45 percent said they did not know.[14] Youth who are coping with the death of another or a terminal illness of their own or a friend can find help in the Bible. All youth, of course, can find guidance in its pages for thinking about the place of death in human existence. The following selected Scriptures will aid discussants.

Impermanence of life—Psalms 90:1-6; 12; 46:1-3; 39:12.
Expressions of anguish—Psalms 130:1-6; 102; John 11:21-27.
Assurance—Psalms 91; 121:1-8; 46:10-11; Romans 8:31-39; 2 Corinthians 12:9.
Future hope—John 14:1-4; 1 Corinthians 15:20-23, 51-56; Romans 6:4; 1 Thessalonians 4:13-18; 1 John 5:11-12; Revelation 21:1-7.

Believers who die are described in the New Testament as being "asleep." Examples are 1 Thessalonians 4:13-14; 5:10; Mark 5:39; and 1 Corinthians 15:51. Such "sleepers" will awaken to everlasting life with Christ, a fact which provides hope for surviving family and friends. "But I would not have you to be ignorant, brethren, concerning them which are asleep; that ye sorrow not, even as others, who have no hope" (1 Thess. 4:13).

Suggested Resources

Charry, Dana. *Mental Health Skills for Clergy.* Valley Forge: Judson Press, 1981.

Grisham, Jack. *Helping Persons Who Grieve.* Birmingham, Ala.: Woman's Missionary Union, n.d. (Also has helpful bibliography, 83-86).

Justice, William G. *When Death Comes.* Nashville: Broadman Press, 1982.

Maples, Donna. *Friends Are for Helping.* Birmingham, Ala.: Women's Missionary Union, 1982.

Oates, Wayne E. *Your Particular Grief.* Philadelphia: Westminster Press, 1981.

Watts, Richard G. *Straight Talk About Death with Young People.* Philadelphia: Westminster Press. 1975. (Direct treatment in language appropriate for young people).

5

Janet Trammel (A)

Although Carl Clayton had been minister to youth at his church in Ardmore for over a year, he felt that this Bible study group on Tuesday evenings was the best of any he had conducted. Fourteen youth and two adult counselors were seated or sprawled comfortably about he and his widowed mother's living room. Carl was particularly pleased that Janet Trammel had come, even if she had arrived late.

Perhaps fifteen minutes into the session the group paused for prayer and the doorbell rang. One of the counselors seated near the door answered it, opening the door to hear an angry man shout, "Where is she? Where is my daughter?" Without another word he burst into the room, grabbed Janet by the arm, and half-dragged her out the door and into his waiting truck. Everyone else seemed frozen in position.

Even as the truck drove away Carl had an anxious feeling of fear for Janet's safety. Though he had no concrete proof, he had suspected for some time that she had been periodically beaten by her father.

Janet's Needs

Shortly after Carl joined the church staff, Yvonne Mitchell, an Ardmore member who worked as a secretary at Hillsborough High School, had given him Janet's name, saying she was someone who needed the church's ministry. Janet had indicated some interest in spiritual matters in informal conversation in the school office. Yvonne also reported Janet to be an adequate student who had experienced no particular school problems.

Carl visited Janet's home a few days later. The Trammel home was located two houses from the church on a small plot of land which made it almost like a small, semirural farm. Carl noticed its run-down condition as he was permitted to step inside the front door.

In his fifties, Mr. Trammel worked as an auto mechanic in a junkyard, was drinking, and essentially ignored Carl. Mrs. Trammel was in her late forties and had only one leg. Carl learned later that when she was in labor with Janet an auto accident en route to the hospital resulted in the amputation. The house was adequately clean and modestly furnished. Janet had two younger brothers and a younger sister who lived at home, and seven other brothers and sisters. Also, there were four friendly dogs, three meowing cats, and some clucking chickens. Being as friendly as possible, Carl invited the entire family to attend Ardmore and extended a special invitation for Janet to participate in the church's youth activities. He received little response except for a smile from Janet.

Subsequently Janet attended a few youth activities, providing Carl and the church youth a chance to get to know her slightly. He also talked with the high school guidance counselor who reported: "I think Mrs. Trammel somehow holds Janet responsible for her amputated leg. She feels that if she had not been in the car at that moment her leg would have been spared." Further, Janet had explained to Carl that her uncertainty about attending church youth activities was because she was required to cook the meals, wash dishes, and do whatever cleaning was done at home. Janet told him that her younger sister had no home responsibilities. Some youth in the church had heard rumors about Janet being mistreated at home. Yvonne Mitchell indicated she suspected the rumors might be true but had no proof. Nevertheless, Janet had been absent from school only three times during the last three months.

Three Incidents

A few weeks after Carl's visit to the Trammels, Mr. Trammel called and surprised Carl by asking him to come over. He wanted to talk to talk to him. When Carl arrived, Mr. Trammel informed him that two of his boys had been caught shoplifting. He had beaten them "with my belt buckle and I guess I'll just have to keep on beating them until they stop it." Carl felt certain Trammel was drunk.

The two boys later told Carl they were hiding out back when he visited and claimed they had worked in the garden that afternoon and had not stolen anything. Carl believed he could see the marks made by the belt buckle. The boys also reported they had stayed away from home that night. Carl checked with the police and juvenile authorities and found no record of any offense.

About three months later Pastor Norman Sheridan reported to Carl that during a deacons' meeting at church the group thought they heard the cries of a girl who seemingly was being beaten, hit, or something from the direction of the Trammel home. (He felt certain it was Janet.) Sheridan called the police, who were unable to take action when no one at the home would admit there was a problem. Carl later noticed a couple of small marks and bruises on Janet's arms when she attended a youth meeting. She said she had been fighting with her brothers.

One Saturday afternoon some weeks later, Carl's doorbell rang. Janet was at the door and, showing him a badly bitten arm, said: "Mr. Clayton, I've been bitten bad on my arm by a dog and I need help." A call to the police about the dog brought them to make a report and advise medical attention. Carl and his mother drove Janet back to her home. The parents were lying in bed resting. Neither one arose. Mr. Trammel ignored the whole matter, and Mrs. Trammel finally glanced at the wound and declared: "We ain't got no doctor. You can take her to the hospital if you want to. We ain't gonna' do nothing." Carl drove Janet to the hospital for treatment. The following day after church Janet said she was a little worried because her parents kept saying she was going to go crazy now. Carl tried to reassure her that she would not. The dog was found on Monday and had a current rabies vaccination.

Bible Study

The youth had been gathering at Carl's house on Tuesdays for Bible study, meeting first at church and carpooling to his home. Janet had been told she could walk to the Bible study if she first cooked supper and cleaned up the kitchen and dishes.

After Mr. Trammel took Janet from Bible study and drove away that night, Carl decided the less said about it the better for Janet. Nevertheless comments were made such as: "Can you believe that?" "I never saw anything like it." "I wonder what's gonna' happen to her now?" Quieting the group, Carl proceeded with a brief period of study, prayer, and refreshments before returning with the youth to the church.

When all the youth had departed from the church, Carl went his car and sat silently. He looked toward Janet's home. Should he go over to the Trammel house? Was Janet in any danger? Would a call to the police be advisable?

Ponderings for Pedagogy

Sometimes called "the family secret" or "hidden crime," child abuse has been increasingly exposed and openly discussed in the past several years. Research, confessional stories, books, and articles have raised the consciousness level of millions of persons. One of the dimensions of that awareness is the realization that most of the abuse of children is inflicted by parents, relatives, and persons known to the child rather than by strangers.

Abuse of another person may take one of four principal forms: physical, emotional, verbal, and/or sexual. *Physical* abuse includes beating, slapping, shaking, burning, and denying the necessities of life such as food. It is injury by nonaccidental means. *Emotional* abuse is the absence of assurance, attention, warmth, affection, and healthy communication. *Verbal* abuse may range from angry yelling, threatening, and belittling to negative teasing and embarrassment. *Sexual* abuse includes fondling, incest, rape, and any other inappropriate sexual behavior forced upon the victim.

Though it may be difficult for people to accept, all human persons have the *potential* to be abusive in one or more of these ways. Perhaps this potential is most obvious in physical abuse where angry words lead to a slap, to a blow which is harder than we intended, making us feel guilty, surprised at what we have done, and alarmed at what we are capable of doing. Paradoxically, abusers can also feel love for their victims.

"No fault" or benign neglect has also been identified to be a form of abuse. Loss of job, home, income, and so forth may simply make it impossible for the caregiver to provide food, shelter, clothing, and money. Such neglect is especially critical in winter if there is no electricity, water, heat, or other basic needs. The caregiver may be so tired he or she cannot care for others. She falls asleep, and children are left without adult supervision. Further, without money one cannot buy cleaning aids to clean the house because food stamps cannot be used for such purchases.[1]

Statistics on abuse are alarming. One in four children will be abused by age eighteen; one in eight girls will have sexual contact/abuse by the same age. Estimates of child abuse are as high as one million per year in the U.S., and thirteen children die each day from this cause. Consider:

- 1,000,000 children/youth run away from home each year.
- 1,000,000 youth suffer neglect or abuse annually.
- 10,000,000 children receive no regular medical care.
- 20,000,000 children/youth under 17 have never seen a dentist.
- Over 17,000,000 children live in debilitating poverty.[2]
- Ninety percent of sexual abuse of children/youth is by someone in the same household.[3]
- Up to one million elderly and dependent adults are abused by their own children or even grandchildren in what geriatric specialist Diana Koin calls "the King Lear Syndrome." (King Lear was abused by his two scheming daughters.)[4]

- Over 7,000 elderly persons commit suicide annually. Many do because of abuse, loneliness, absence of contact with family, and absence of joy from life.[5]
- Fourteen years is the average beginning age of child prostitutes, of which fifty one percent are boys and forty-nine percent girls.
- Over five billion dollars was made by the child sex industry in 1982.[6]

Even pregnant mothers do not escape physical abuse in American society. In a study of prenatal clinics, the March of Dimes reported that one of every twelve pregnant women was beaten by her male partner. Spokesperson Betsy Berkheimer-Credair said: "Battered women are four times more likely to deliver low-birthweight babies and twice as likely to miscarry," and these "babies are more likely to be born with defects and more than 40 times more likely to die during the first month of life."[7] Such violence is made more "acceptable" by a legal system which includes such jurists as Illinois Criminal Judge Christy Berkos who explained a lenient sentence given to notorious plumber-rapist Brad Lieberman for five rapes by saying: "Lieberman had done things that did hurt the women, but fortunately he did not hurt the women physically by breaking their heads or the other things we see. He didn't cut their breasts off, for instance."[8]

The National Institute of Mental Health has recognized the problem of sexual abuse of adolescents, including date rape, in its publication "The Sexual Victimization of Adolescents."[9]

Jan Lundy suggests several steps for dealing with abuse: consider confidentiality and legal issues; believe and relate to the victim; relate to the family to protect the victim and move the whole family toward therapy; and give a message of hope and redemption. These steps should be followed for a life-long healing process.[10]

Search Institute found that twenty-five percent of the 8,165 adolescents which they studied worried "somewhat," "quite a bit," or "very much" that one of their parents would hit them so hard that they would be hurt badly. Remember that subjects of this study are children of church families. After listing twenty-three possible symptoms of child abuse and ten physical symptoms, Merton and Irene Strommen recommend seeking help from community agencies and group counseling for the abusers.[11] They also report that Murray Straus's research conducted for the U.S. Government of 1,146 families revealed that approximately fourteen of every one hundred children between the ages of three and seventeen experience an average of 10.5 episodes of violence each year.[12]

Themes

The major theme in this case is obviously the treatment of Janet Trammel and her brothers. The unavoidable legal implications and requirements upon adults who are related to the family, including Carl Clayton and Pastor Sheridan, are attached to this situation. Also this is a family in great distress. Where is care and love in a group when it is so enmeshed that no one wants to "tell"? Additionally there are the many roles of persons who know and relate to Janet: school secretary, counselor, pastor, Carl, youth group, and church adults. What is the nature and extent of their obligation to this unhappy family?

Another theme is the parenting style of the Trammels. A powerful factor is the apparently latent feelings of resentment held by Mrs. Trammel toward Janet, a resentment which she may also be transferring to her other children.

Group Leadership

How is "child abuse" to be legally defined? In 1974 the United States Congress passed the "Child Abuse Prevention and Treatment Act." Included in its provisions was the following definition: "Child abuse is the physical or mental injury, sexual abuse, negligent treatment, or maladjustment of a child under circumstances which indicate that the child's welfare or health was harmed or threatened thereby." Each state will have its own legal definition of child abuse. If possible, it will be helpful to secure and use the one from your own state for the discussion.

Focus group attention on the legal definition given above or on your state's definition. A poster, printed sheet, or transparency on an overhead projector may be used to display your definition. Then ask the group if they are aware of or know about any cases of child abuse. It may be helpful to identify the four types of abuse discussed in the preceding section. If they appear to be willing, participants can comment on their knowledge of such specific abuse. Experience shows that introducing and discussing the nature of abuse is essential if the procedure suggested in the next paragraph is chosen for use.

You might consider conducting a personal survey of the group. You can suggest the survey by saying something like: "I hope you feel free enough to participate in what I realize is a 'delicate' and confidential 'research' experiment. I want give each of you a sheet of paper and ask that you write 'yes' or 'no' indicating that you are or have been a victim of child abuse by another. Fold the paper in half and pass them in." In groups with whom I've used this case, I have found that 5 to 25 percent of participants identify themselves as victims of abuse. The results of the survey aid in knowing the extent of the problem and the type of interest within the group. They need not be shared with the group.

While this voluntary response process is going on, focus attention on the following figures which you have previously recorded on a chalkboard or newsprint: one million, one million, ten million, twenty million. (Turning to this activity will enable persons to respond to the survey more unobtrusively.) As you speak, fill in the identifying information for the U.S. as it is given under statistics provided earlier. Is it reasonable to anticipate that such children are being deprived of their chance to grow into happy adults? Will there be lasting effects?

Ask discussants to assume that they are newspaper reporters and have them identify the "facts" in this case. Help them stick strictly to facts without adding any assumptions, descriptions, or conclusions. Another approach is to have participants act as police investigators in order to get the facts.

Issues

After the persons are identified and facts are recorded, lead the group to suggest what they see as major *issues.* Issues which have been considered by other groups are: child abuse, maternal (and perhaps paternal) rejection and anger, legal issues, congregational involvement, coping with marginal poverty (deprivation, hopelessness), pastor's role, role of the school, and difficulties in rearing a large family.

It can be worthwhile to follow consideration of issues with the question of whether or not Janet really is a problem at home, as her parents may feel. Is she "suckering" Carl into believing only her side of the story? Does she really understand or care about her parents' feelings, problems, and struggles? Should she be made to feel more sympathetic toward them? Why are her parents responding as they are? What are they feeling? Why?

This case calls for some *action* by Carl. Ask, What should Carl do? Possible actions will be affected by how the case is presented. If participants have read only the portion of the case which ends with Carl sitting in his car pondering what to do, here are some possibilities: do nothing, call the police, go to the house, find Pastor Sheridan and go to the Trammel home, pray, get congregational involvement, or notify a child welfare agency.

An interesting and usually productive technique is to select or secure volunteers to role-play a possible visit by Carl alone, or with Pastor Sheridan, to the Trammel home. The conversation should take place with Mr. and Mrs. Trammel and perhaps include Janet. This interchange can heighten and clarify issues and relationships. Secure actors who can simulate the tensions within this family.

Use of (B) Case

At this point in the discussion it is a good technique to distribute the remainder of the case for reading by the group. Ask them to look up at you when they have finished reading "Janet Trammel (B)."

Janet Trammel (B)

After returning to his home, Carl called the pastor to let him know about the incident. Pastor Sheridan said Carl was right in not going to the Trammel home because he knew the family well enough to know it would just have made things worse for Janet. This helped Carl to sleep a little better.

The next morning Carl received a telephone call from Juvenile Hall inquiring about any information he might have about Janet Trammel and her family situation. The official explained:

> We have Janet Trammel in custody here (since she is not yet eighteen). Her parents have filed a complaint saying they could not control her, and she was brought in by them late last night. It may sound strange, but they said she had gotten "too Christian," too involved in your church, and refused to obey them. They say they do not want her and want her to be placed under the jurisdiction of the court. A preliminary hearing is set for Thursday. The probation officer would like for you to be there. The girl asked us to call you.

Carl shared what he knew about Janet, said he would be present on Thursday, and hung up. For a moment he sat in stunned silence. He called Pastor Sheridan who agreed also to be present for the hearing.

At the hearing a social worker reported that the parents did not want Janet in their home. They said she was too involved in the church and that they could control her. They simply wanted her out of the home. The probation officer informed the judge that all preliminary evidence indicated the home might be undesirable. Seeming to agree, the judge set a trial date for late the next month and directed that Janet could be placed in a temporary foster home. Janet's parents were not present.

A foster home was located on Thursday afternoon, and Janet moved in. When her parents did not bring her clothes to Juvenile Hall a court order was issued; the clothing finally arrived the following Thursday. In the meantime, the foster mother bought a suit for Janet to wear to school on Friday. The foster mother was convinced someone tried to follow her as she drove back from picking up Janet's clothing at Juvenile Hall.

The other Trammel children apparently did not know Janet was in the custody of the court, having been told she ran away. Janet shared one class with her younger sister; they reportedly sat in the same classroom on Friday without speaking but with an occasional sniffle. Several attempts were made by the Trammel children to locate the foster home. The boys peeked in church windows to search for Janet during youth events and came in to ask Carl where she was.

Janet had asked that the probation officer and foster mother see that she didn't have to go back home. She was in church the next Sunday morning after receiving her clothes.

The judge's final decision could come as early as next month.

Guiding Further Discussion

Following a few minutes for reading the new material, lead the group to talk about these considerations:

(1) What new options do you now see for Carl? Can he do anything now that you had not considered before? What?

(2) What resources of grace do you see being available for helping Janet? Her family? Consider the guidance counselor, prayer, youth group, congregation, public agencies, and other relatives.

(3) How would you assess Carl's handling of the situation? You may want to have the entire group make a "pro" list and then a "con" list. Using the whole group for each listing will help avoid creating any divisions within the group.

(4) What can we learn from this case? Consider the following:

a. An important fact is that all parents are *potential* abusers, beginning with slaps, words, harsh treatment, and so forth which can become more severe and hurtful than was ever intended.

b. Church people find it hard to admit that abuse exists in their midst, in the "good families" of their congregation and community.

c. In most states either suspicion or knowledge of child abuse *must* be reported to police or social work authorities; it is not optional.

d. The minister of youth may be the first person to learn about abuse. The abused youth in many cases may tell the youth minister first.

Sharon Wolfe Sanders, psychiatric social worker, has suggested to youth workers a "to do list" of ideas for helping in cases of child abuse, whether it is actual, suspected, or potential.

● Help meet physical needs of child and family, especially in poor and disadvantaged families. Of course, move first to ensure immediate physical safety and health if it is required. If conditions represent or raise suspicions of abuse, notify authorities.

- Teach parenting skills to adults and youth.
- Provide support groups for "stressed-out" parents and youth. "Mother's Day Out" provided by your church can provide a few hours of free time forparents and reduce stress.
- Provide child care during a retreat involving parents.
- Provide a confidential hotline through the church.
- Keep abusive parents in touch with "Parents Anonymous" in your area or with another similar support group.
- Teach what is appropriate behavior for age groups. Train age-group workers, potential workers, and even youth who baby-sit what is "normal" behavior for the age group with which they are working or relating.
- Teach and discuss what is *acceptable* discipline. Use discussion groups, films, resource persons, and so forth.
- During a retreat or "special day out with you," ask youth to write on paper and put in a box some topics or issues of concern to them. Discuss these topics anonymously in an appropriate forum.
- Use music which communicates "I am OK." Do not overload youth with lyrics which are heavy with unworthiness and self-critical themes.
- Deal with making choices, particularly "What do I do when I have made a bad choice?" Provide some processes for arriving at choices.
- Do not criticize or be judgmental of youth's parents. Even abusive parents may represent what the child sees as the only present hope for warmth, security, and even love.
- Don't promise confidentiality. Promise responsible handling of information in consultation with the person(s) involved.
- Use their words to talk about the abuse, even if the slang is objectionable to you. This is particularly crucial in cases of sexual abuse.
- Keep a record of what is happening and any involvement you have in it. This may become a valuable legal record for you, as well as a source of guidance for ways in which you can help.
- Teach children and youth that no one has a "right" to their body. Teach children that going to, being picked up, or being held or hugged by another person is their choice—not an obligation.
- Inform parents about factors which can produce abuse. They include stress, isolation, parenting problems, mental problems, high expectations, role reversals, and abusers who were victims themselves.
- Know when to refer a case. Cases of family violence should be handled only by persons with extensive background in such intervention. It is a complex, difficult problem. Referral is almost always best.
- Train and inform persons in your church, agency, or organization that all of us are involved in family ministry.

Suggested Resources

Child Abuse Project, Education Commission of the United States, Suite 300, 1860 Lincoln Street, Denver, CO 80295.

Dolan, Edward F., Jr. *Child Abuse.* New York: Franklin Watts, 1980.

Garbarino, James and S. H. Stocking, eds. *Protecting Children from Abuse and Neglect.* San Francisco: Jossey-Bass Publishers, 1980.

National Center for the Prevention and Treatment of Child Abuse and Neglect, 4200 East 9th Avenue, Denver, CO 80262.

National Committee for Prevention of Child Abuse. 111 E. Wacker Drive, Suite 510, Chicago, IL 60601.

Schneider, Andrew. *The Children's Rights Movement.* Garden City: Anchor Press, 1977.

Tower, Cynthia Crosson. *Understanding Child Abuse and Neglect.* Boston: Allyn and Bacon, 1986.

Van Hassett, V. B., Morrison, R. L., Bellack, A. S., and Hersen, M., editors. *Handbook of Family Violence.* New York: Plenum Press, 1988.

6

Freedom to Grow

As Mary Johnson sat by the telephone, she could hear her fifteen-year-old daughter Katie crying in the next room.[1] The night before, Katie's date, Mike Fedson, had been picked up on suspicion of drunk driving as he was bringing Katie home from a local high school party. Mike was eighteen. He was taken to police headquarters, and the couple with whom Katie and Mike were double dating had brought her home at 3:00 a.m.

When Katie came down to breakfast that morning, she told her mother she was sorry about worrying her so much the night before. Katie said that if she had called from the police station she was afraid her parents would have been even more concerned. Mary was still quite upset and told Katie she was going to call the party chaperons. Mary reminded Katie that when she had agreed to let her go to the party with an older boy, she had been assured that no alcohol was allowed at the party. Mary told Katie that she was considering a meeting of the parents of the young people in Katie's crowd.

At this point, Katie had broken down in tears and said, "Why do you want to embarrass me? It's not any of your business what the other kids do. I don't drink. I think it's stupid. Everybody else drinks, and what I say about it wouldn't make any difference.

"Look, Mother, Mike had a few beers in the parking lot. He wasn't drunk. On our way home the police stopped him to check his driver's license, and they smelled alcohol on his breath. That's all. It's not so serious. We weren't in an accident or anything like that. You're blowing this whole thing up. If you call all my friends' parents and make a big thing out of all this, I won't have any friends left at all, and I won't have another date for the rest of my life!" Katie ran into her room crying and slammed the door.

Mary Johnson was still determined to call one of the adult chaperons for the party and learn why drinking had been allowed. Ted Mallory, a chaperon, responded with cold, crisp logic: "My wife and I were asked to be present at the party, admit no alcoholic beverages, and generally supervise the kids there. What goes on out in the parking lot is none of our business. This goes on at all the parties. You've got to give the kids some room to grow up. It's crazy to think about supervising them every minute. The seniors will be in jobs or college in a few more months. It's better to let them learn to handle the alcohol now than when they're completely on their own. We're forty-five miles from the state line. If we don't let the teenagers drink here, they'll drive into the next state where the legal age is only eighteen, three years younger than here, and get killed driving home. Come on, Mary, I know you and Bruce both drink socially. Why should it be different for the kids?" Ted Mallory hung up the phone with a definite "click."

Mary later said she really wanted to tell Mallory off. "Sure, he was logical," Mary reasoned, "but the blunt truth of the matter is that letting those kids buy liquor is as illegal and irresponsible as Mike's driving when he had been drinking. I'm not trying to raise Katie in a cocoon, but kids need some clear limits until they are mature enough to make responsible decisions. Allowing them to break the law and slip around the rules isn't the way to go about it."

After the call to Ted Mallory, Mary sat back and tried to sort out what she saw as her options. She remembered that Katie's father had been equally disturbed before he left for the office this morning. He was quite angry with Mike Fedson and suggested that Katie should never be allowed to go out with him again. Bruce told Mary, "Maybe our decision to let Katie date an older boy or go to these parties was a mistake after all. I don't know if Katie asked him not to drink or if that would have made any difference. I want Katie to know that we trust her, but it's not fair to let her get into situations she can't handle at her age."

Mary was hesitant to tell Katie she could neither go to the parties nor date Mike anymore. Katie had been dating him for several weeks; he was from a nice family and had always seemed courteous. Katie was just beginning to gain some confidence in herself and seemed to be thriving on the special "prestige" of dating an older boy. Mary thought, *If Bruce and I tell Katie she can no longer see Mike, it could put a barrier between us. Forcing Katie to see Mike in secret might turn into an exciting game that would be terribly destructive to her relationship with us. We've tried to give Katie more freedom than our parents ever gave us. However, maybe Bruce is right. The old-fashioned limits might be the best thing for Katie.*

I guess what is really underneath the issue of Katie's dating is my wider concern for the whole crowd of teenagers who not only see drinking as a smart thing to do but can attend organized parties where they are allowed to drink freely, even if it is outside and not inside. I don't want to be the kind of mother who constantly interferes with her child's life, but I do want to do the most loving and responsible thing for Katie as well as the other youngsters involved. Maybe what our minister said at church on Sunday about the difference between real freedom and what it means to really love someone is at stake here. Wouldn't a meeting of some of the parents to talk over the issues be better than restricting Katie? Or would she be so hurt by my taking a step like this, that it would do more harm to Katie than good? What if I find out that it doesn't make any difference to the other parents?

The logic of Ted Mallory and sound of Katie sobbing in the next room made Mary hesitate before she started to look up the first number.

Ponderings for Pedagogy

A 1986 poll of a representative sample of America's high achievers in high school probably produced few surprises for experienced workers with youth. Seventy-seven percent of the youth reported alcohol was regularly used in many weekend activities, and 35 percent reported some students took drugs regularly before school. The use of alcohol is so pervasive that it has become the major leisure activity of a large percentage of both adults and youth in many societies. For example, England recently held a national conference on alcohol abuse in the workplace and has heard the charge that there is a "conspiracy of silence" between the boardroom and shop floor concerning alcohol and drug addiction. Why? Because the executives are too often excessive drinkers themselves.[2] They also reported that about 100,000 persons were convicted each year for drink and driving offenses.[3]

The "drug of choice" by youth is alcohol. Social acceptance and use make it difficult to combat and increase pressure to use it. Thus, alcoholic children are being found in fourth, fifth, and sixth grades. *The Weekly Reader* for elementary schools reported in a 1988 survey that more than 30 percent of fourth graders said they were pressured by peers to drink alcoholic beverages. Ninety-two percent of all 1987 high school seniors admitted having some experience with alcohol and nearly 40 percent said they had five or more drinks in a row during the week prior to the survey.[4] In the U.S. there are an estimated 13 million alcoholics. Alcoholism is a disease which kills 100,000 to 200,000 Americans annually, and 28.6 million children have alcoholic parents.[5]

Many congressmen are alarmed by the fact that drunk driving has become the leading killer of youth ages fifteen to twenty. In 1989 former U.S. Surgeon General Everett Koop was urged by ninety-nine senators and a unanimous House of Representatives to do something about drunk driving. He proposed increased taxes, restrictions on advertising, and reduction of the permissible blood alcohol level from

0.10 to 0.04 percent. Federal taxes on beer and wine have not been changed since 1951—making a six-pack of beer cost less than a similar amount of soft drinks.[6]

The comsumption of alcoholic beverages costs society about twice as much as drinkers pay in alcohol taxes. A study by the Rand Corporation found these costs reflected in auto accidents, sick leave, and other expenses. The researchers reported that alcohol costs society forty-eight cents per ounce which is more than double the current average state and federal tax of twenty-three cents per ounce of absolute alcohol. They recommended doubling the federal tax on alcohol.[7]

The seriousness with which alcohol consumption is beginning to be viewed has been furthered by the work of such groups as MADD (Mothers Against Drunk Driving) and SADD (Students Against Drunk Driving). New laws are being enacted by some states which raise the legal drinking age. A study by the Justice Department shows similar actions to reduce the number of arrests of young people for drunk driving. The study also found that 88 percent of people arrested for drunk driving and 95 percent of those jailed are men.[8]

Two concerns about alcohol have arisen within the alcohol industry itself. One centers on the negative publicity about drunkenness and its impact on society. This concern has produced two responses, one being the liquor industry's slogan "know when to say when" and their open campaign to select a "designated driver" to drive a group of drinkers home.

The other industry concern is that 1989 showed a decrease of 4.2 percent in alcohol consumption, an eighteen-year low. In response, the alcohol industry has increased its efforts to sell to overseas customers, especially Japanese.[9] In addition, the Distilled Spirits Council of the U.S. produced a special "Reporter's Guide to the Liquor Industry" which suggests how reporters should treat alcohol stories. For example, *alcoholic drinks* should be alcohol drink and *hard liquor* called just liquor. *Booze* is to be avoided. What is their rationale? "It's unfair to place a derogatory label on liquor, a beverage that plays an important role in many social and religious events."[10]

While the greatest volume of alcoholic beverages is sold in large urban areas, there is also evidence of growing use in rural areas. In 1983 an Alcohol Student Survey was administered to 650 students in grades seven to twelve in a small city of 25,000 and the surrounding county of 53,000 in a Middle Atlantic state.[11] The nearest metropolitan area was over one hundred miles away, and the area was isolated on three sides by mountain ranges. Prevalence of alcohol use was quite high, only 17 percent reported never having taken a drink. Rural youth are "catching up" to the drinking habits of their urban peers. Further, religious affiliation/activity was not a persistent predictor of drinking practices. (The survey population was relatively high in Baptists, Mennonites, and Church of the Brethren.) School grade level was the most powerful predictor. "The findings of the present study indicate that the prevalence of alcohol use in a small mid-Atlantic city and county is quite high. . . . It is clear that alcohol is a drug problem for rural young people."[12]

While the obvious focus of this case is on the drinking of alcoholic beverages by youth, other themes and concerns should not be overlooked. The tensions between freedom and maturity levels may be explored, particularly for Katie Johnson. What amount of freedom is appropriate for a fifteen-year-old? How can parents determine that level? Another theme is the responsibility of youth leaders for the behavior of youth at chaperoned youth activities. Additional themes include legal considerations, trust levels, parental guidelines for acceptable behavior by their children, and the consistency of parental drinkers who tell their children not to drink.

These and other themes have emerged in the case's use with youth, parents, dialogues between parents and youth, and trialogues (parents, youth, and leaders). It has also proved helpful in creating meaningful analysis of the relational and social systems which exist among family members. The authors of the case indicate that it has been especially useful in a retreat or family camp setting. Their emphasis has been on values involved in the case and the way in which parents influence the values of their children.

Group Leadership

One way to begin is by asking the group members to identify the persons in the case and to provide data on what they know about him/her. To have a variety consider: (1) Distributing sheets of paper with names, asking group members to jot down descriptions, and then discuss the case. (2) Having youth pretape each person in the case on video with different youth playing each one. (3) Using a preprepared poster for each person in the case. Let the group suggest characteristics or traits of each and record them on the poster. Since little is known about Bruce, you may want to list Mary and Bruce together and list others separately.

Issues

Ask: What are the concerns and attitudes of each person involved? Suggestions might reflect some of the following, which have been considered by other study groups.

Mary and Bruce
Illegal
Need for limits
Fairness
Older boy as date
Trust Katie
Katie's safety
Loving and responsible actions

Katie
Friendship
Acceptance
Prestige
Peers
Threatened

Mike Fedson
Guilty?
Embarrassed?
Care?
Do we know?

Ted Mallory
Not responsible for parking lot
Goes on at parties
Soon be in college
Learn to handle
    State line—danger
    Johnsons' drinking

Guide the group to examine *why* the person has these particular feelings or concerns. What is behind or the basis for them? Do you feel each concern is justified? Why? Are there ones with which you disagree? Why?

Ask the discussants to identify the issues in the case by thinking first of a word like consistency and then expressing the issue in the form of a question. Some issues which have resulted from using this technique with other groups are:

    1. *Maturity*—Should parents allow youth to be in situations which are beyond the ability of the youth to control? Or beyond their maturity level for the decision making which is required?

    2. *Consistency*—Do drinking parents have the moral right to restrict the drinking of their children? To what extent?

    3. *Responsibility versus freedom*—In such matters as drinking, how can parents achieve a balance between parental responsibility and youth freedom?

    4. *Freedom versus license*—Can Katie be given freedom while avoiding the risk of its becoming license? How? What are the differences between real freedom and license?

    5. *Legal*—Is Ted Mallory legally liable for breaking the law regarding underage drinking? Is he liable in case of a resulting accident? Did he guarantee parents (specifically Mary) there would be no drinking? Does Mike Fedson have any liability?

    6. *Youth versus adults*—How does the "united front" of youth ("everyone else drinks. . . . It's not any of your business. . . .") versus a "fragmented front" of most parents affect parenting? Affect youth?

    7. *Drinking*—Is drinking itself an issue? It may be noted that the 1986

"Who's Who Among American High School Students" survey of juniors and seniors found that 32 percent said they had never tried alcohol and 81 percent had never tried marijuana or cocaine.

8. *Values*—Robert and Alice Evans, authors of this case, suggest that some major values include freedom, responsibility of each person, trust, love, and caring. They suggest several guidelines for loving which have developed from their use of the case with a number of groups:
- Trust as a foundation
- Mutual respect
- Mutual responsibility
- Promotion of freedom
- Compassionate acknowledgment of needs, promises, and failures

Mary's Options

At the end of this case, Mary Johnson faces the dilemma of whether to take action, and if so, what specific action would be best? Some options to be considered by the group are:
- Dismiss and forget it. Doing nothing is always an option.
- Forbid Katie to date Mike Fedson or any other boy older than she.
- Talk with Mike Fedson.
- Seek a covenant with Katie and Mike about drinking.
- Volunteer as a chaperon for the next dance.
- Approach and work with school officials about her concerns.
- Meet informally with some other parents to talk over some of the issues and ways for parents to cope.

Two other ideas can be helpful. First, ask if there is a place in this case for intervention by the church and/or pastor as a resource of grace for Mary and Katie? How? What form would it take?

Another technique is to use a brief role play. Secure two telephones (disconnected) and ask one participant to play the role of Mary Johnson and the other the minister of youth at her church. Have the two persons sit several feet apart with their backs toward one another. Assume you are the minister of youth at Mary Johnson's church, and she calls you. She explains her dilemma and asks for your advice. What would you say to her?

As the role play proceeds, intervene at a time of good interchanges between the participants. Lead the group to evaluate the counsel given Mary by her minister of youth. Conclude by leading a discussion about what you (discussants) would want to say/tell each person in the case.

Biblical Sources

Among the Scripture references which the group can study are the following: Leviticus 10:9; Proverbs 20:2; Isaiah 28:7-8; Luke 1:15; Romans 13:12-14; Ephesians 5:15-18.

Suggested Resources

Alcohol

Bean, Margaret H. *Alcohol and Adolescents: Identifying and Managing the Problems.* Minneapolis: Johnson Institute, 1982.

Brook, Judith S., and Lettier, Dave J., et al. *Alcohol and Substance Abuse in Adolescence.* New York: Haworth Press, 1985.

Christian Life Commission of Southern Baptist Convention, 901 Commerce Street, Suite 550, Nashville, TN 37203. The Christian Life Commission also has resources on teen-parent concerns.

Journal of Studies on Alcohol, Inc. New Haven, Conn. Some journal issues deal with drinking and driving.

Mendelson, Jack H., Nancy K. Mells, *Alcohol: Use and Abuse in America.* Boston: Little, Brown, 1985.

National Clearing House for Alcohol and Drug Information, P. O. Box 2345, Rockville, MD 20852.

Sisk, Ronald D. *Alcoholic Awareness: A Guide for Teenagers and Their Parents.* Nashville: Christian Life Commission of the Southern Baptist Convention, 1983.

Many large school districts employ a full-time director for drug and alcohol information who could serve as a resource person. Temperance Leagues, MADD, Alcoholics Anonymous, Board of Health, and other such groups are also sources of information on the problems of alcohol.

Parent-Teens

Dobson, James C. *Parenting Isn't for Cowards.* Waco, Tex.: Word Books, 1987.

Elkind, David. *All Grown Up and No Place to Go.* Reading, Mass.: Addison-Wesley Publishing Co., 1984.

Peck, Terry A. *Parenting in the Minister's Home.* Nashville: Convention Press, 1988.

Powell, Lane. *The Dating Book.* Nashville: Convention Press, 1989.

Strommen, Merton and A. Irene. *Five Cries of Parents.* San Francisco: Harper and Row, 1985.

7

Westport Grass

"Keeping her at home is the least I can do. She'll run away if I do it. If I don't she'll just keep going down a crooked road in a wheelbarrow," Mrs. Katy James said.

"I'll get out of here and go to California. She thinks I'm a kid. I'm seventeen!" Linda James said.

Nancy Heiser knew when the 6:15 p.m. call came that Linda James was in trouble again.[1] As a youth leader, she had known Linda as an obstinate member of the Y.P.F. (Young People's Fellowship) for two years.

"Mrs. Heiser? This is Katy James. Would you come right over?"

Nancy said, "I have a meeting of the Y.P.C. (Council of the Y.P.F.) Could this wait until 9:30 or so, after the meeting?"

"No, my husband Ronald will be back about 10:00, and we need to get this thing settled. We need you now." Nancy called the president of the fellowship and told him to go ahead without her. "I'll get there when I can," she said.

Nancy drove the three miles to Westport Vista where the James family lived. She was trying to recall what she knew about the family. They lived in a small apartment in Westport Village, one of the better suburbs of town, so that Linda could attend Westport High School. Their older children were in all kinds of trouble. Harry left Fort Dixon without leave and now was evidently an alcoholic somewhere nearby, because Linda spoke every once in a while about him. Willa, too, had been rather wild at Central High. A rumor circulated that she was arrested for prostitution during her senior year.

Linda was a striking girl with beautiful features and a good figure. Most of her friends were older. That's how she had first come to the youth group—with Jim Thatcher, who was a senior at the time. Jim had graduated and gone to college, but Linda kept coming off and on to the group. For one thing, Centenary Church had an excellent softball team, and Linda was a good player. However, Nancy suspected that Linda came mostly to be with the boys.

Sam, one of the fellows in the youth group, mentioned Linda's use of drugs to Nancy. Nancy took the initiative and asked Linda to eat out at the Pancake House after a game. That was more than a month ago. Nancy made an offer to help Linda. "If you're taking drugs and want to stop, we can get you help. Your parents don't have to know," she said.

Linda had responded to this offer with diffidence: "You're a gossip, and I don't need you." Strangely enough, though, Linda was regular in attendance at church and Y.P.F. for a month or more.

As Nancy arrived at the James's house, she could hear Linda yelling, "You won't keep me from anything!"

"Oh, come in, Mrs. Heiser. Thank you for coming," Mrs. James greeted her as she took Nancy's raincoat. Quickly Linda explained why the confrontation occurred. "Mother found some grass and pills in my drawer," she said.

"I was putting some things away for Linda and saw it," Mrs. James offered.

"Mother, it was all wrapped up in a bag. You had absolutely no right to look. I am entitled to my privacy. Don't you think so?" Linda asked.

"What did you do?" asked Nancy.

"My first thought was to show it to Ronald. He'd probably beat her and call the police, too. Ronald and I don't talk much. With me working days and him working 'swing' we just don't. I told Linda that she can't go out for two weeks—except to church and youth group, of course."

"And I told you I'll just leave!" Linda walked (or rather stalked) around the room.

Nancy wanted to shake some sense into Linda, but instead ignored her and spoke again to Mrs. James.

"Why did you think punishment like this would be the right thing?" Nancy asked.

"Dr. Ayers was counseling Linda last year. She went several times to one of his groups, but quit because she said it was all girls. Anyway he said for me to keep her home as punishment. That's something she doesn't like to do—stay home."

"Mommy's always doing what other people say," Linda chimed in. "That's the way it is right now. She doesn't care whether I pop stuff or not. Do you know what she said? She said, 'Linda, what will people think if you get arrested for using drugs?' "

"Where is the marijuana now?" asked Nancy.

"Oh," Mrs. James responded, "I put it back in her drawer, and the pills, too."

"Let's get it out," Nancy said.

When they went to the bedroom, Linda gestured angrily that they should leave her things alone. Mrs. James opened the drawer. She took out a rather large bag and handed it to Nancy quickly, wiped her hands in a rather loud, clapping motion, and said: "I sure am glad to hand this over to you."

Nancy opened the bag and discovered two parcels—one held several hundred red capsules, the other at least a pound of what looked like marijuana. "I had no idea you were talking this much," she said.

"That's not much," Linda retorted. "Put it back."

Ponderings for Pedagogy

Few people would argue with the observation that the 1960s were a watershed in changing American social attitudes and life-styles, revolving around a centerpiece of freedom and pleasure reflected in the slogan "If it feels good, do it!" Whatever else may be said about the ethos, it resulted in an increased use of drugs and alcohol—which are producing bitter fruit in many contemporary families. The "proof" lies in the announcement by George Gallup, Jr., that in 1989 Americans for the first time pointed to drugs as the number one problem facing the nation.

The seriousness of drug use, abuse, and sales now transcends the individual addict/user and has become a deepening crisis for the world. Ben Johnson's Olympic record is expunged. The reason? His use of steroids. Panama's Noreiga is under indictment for drug trafficking. Judges and political leaders in Colombia have been threatened and publicly assassinated by the Medellian drug cartel. Fidel Castro has executed a longtime army leader and supporter and sentenced others to long prison terms for selling drugs. Sicily remains in the grip of Mafia crime bosses whose chief source of revenue is illegal drugs. This crisis led President Bush to "declare war" on dealers and users and to appoint William Bennett as America's first "Drug Czar." A relatively new phrase in our vocabulary is "substance abuse."

Drawing from several sources, Ray Conner reports these facts about alcohol and drugs:

- An estimated 80 percent or more of all Americans are "hooked" on some type of drug.
- Half of high school coaches believe drug-alcohol use by student athletes is a very serious problem and getting worse.
- Each day 5,000 persons in the U.S. try cocaine for the first time. At least one-third of these will become addicts.
- There are at least twenty-four million cocaine users in the U.S. of which 400,000 need clinical attention, says Dr. Ronald K. Siegel, University of California School of Medicine.
- National Institute of Drug Abuse reports that sleeping pills kill 5,000 people annually and cause an additional 25,000 hospital emergency room visits.

- Over sixty million prescriptions for the tranquilizer Valium are written each year.
- National Institute of Mental Health claims that ten and a half million persons in the U.S. have a substance abuse problem.[2]

The National Household Survey on Drug Use reported that its 1988 fall survey revealed fewer casual users; growing cocaine addiction; a rise in heavy users of cocaine and crack since 1985; and 72 million Americans—37 percent of the population—have tried one illicit drug in their lifetime.[3]

The drug problem in the U.S. has led to the development of an enormous number of organizations and programs which attempt to prevent child and teen use. The U.S. Department of Health and Human Services has produced both a parent's guide and leader's guide called *10 Steps to Help Your Child Say "NO."* Other examples include SPARK, a counseling program in New York schools, the Chicago Youth Development Project founded by the Ford Foundation in 1960, and Project CLASP at Stanford University.[4]

Recent research shows that students are much more likely to use drugs *away* from, rather than on, school grounds. Researchers at Colorado State University found that "only about one in ten students has ever used drugs at school" and only 12 percent had ever used drugs at school events, such as dances or sporting events. Twenty-eight percent of drug use occurred at parties, 31 percent at night with friends, and 18 percent while driving around.[5]

Conner suggests six ideas for combatting the drug problem among children and youth:

- Have drug education at home, school, and church.
- Petition the media to stop "glamorizing" drug use, including alcohol and tobacco.
- Provide good adult role models.
- Know facts about drugs; watch for symptoms of use.
- Get professional help if needed.
- Encourage "positive peer pressure" away from drug use.[6]

This case and the previous case, "Freedom to Grow," both highlight the drug problem which, of course, includes alcohol. Also, they both point to the more fundamental search of persons for some way to lower, if not eliminate by chemical means, the effects of unwanted feelings of stress, isolation, discouragement, anxiety, conflict, and pain. From coffee, to aspirin, to Valium and Elevil, our society has become filled with drugs. This case shows the problems within the life of one youth, one family, and one church congregation.

The most obvious theme in this case is drug possession and use.

However, other themes center on the social system of the James family. The relationship between the father and mother, along with the quality of their communications, can be examined. The impact of such conditions on Linda are part of this system of relationships.

The church is directly linked to this case through the youth leader Nancy Heiser. Her actions and use of resources can be potential channels of grace and will symbolize and represent Christian ministry to the James family. What forms of youth ministry should be considered? Should Nancy attempt to have the Centenary Church congregation become a resource? If so, in what way(s)? By involving the pastor?

Freedom versus responsibility is reflected in Linda's actions. Being free to choose, she has acted to involve herself and others in her choice. The presence of and knowledge about the drugs bring both of Linda's parents and Nancy into the events.

While drug laws vary among states, most have strict regulations and penalties regarding possession and/or use of illegal drugs. Therefore, both Nancy and Mrs. James may have some legal obligations regarding their knowledge and consequent actions.

The task of the church in attempting to help people in crisis is yet another theme. What is the nature and extent of the church's responsibility to minister to such people? How can Christian belief be "fleshed out" in helping ways?

Louis Weeks, academic dean and professor at Louisville Presbyterian Theological Seminary, has led discussions about this case a number of times with youth ministers, musicians, and educators. He has also used it with parents and youth and believes it raises such issues as Christian responsibility and the application of law. The following suggestions for group leadership are from such teaching/discussion sessions.

Group Leadership

Begin by asking if all *facts* in the case are clear. Does anyone need to ask a question about the facts? Is everyone clear on the information supplied in the case? If necessary, discuss briefly any facts not clearly understood.

Most groups find it helpful to *identify the persons* in the case, adding information under each name as it is listed. Help discussants to identify not only the persons involved but the particular feelings, attitudes, or even failures of each person. Remain with what is known, avoiding too much conjecture. While there are three main characters, the minor characters should also be noted (Ronald, Dr. Ayers, siblings, boyfriend, and so forth).

Identify the *major issues* in the case. Groups have suggested issues such as Linda's privacy, legal matters, moral issues, avoidance by Katy and Nancy, authority, communication, right to intervention by Nancy as a church representative, Nancy ignoring Linda, and theological issues (sin, free will, and punishment for wrong-doing).

Lead identify the group to *alternatives for action*. Their suggestions may be enriched by some of those which were listed earlier. Alternative actions could be to pray, call police, contact Ronald James, put drugs back, take the drugs, disengage by leaving, call Dr. Ayers, sit down and talk, or do nothing.

One good way to examine the value of these possible actions is to ask persons to work in groups of two or three for a brief time and develop answers for these questions: (1) If you were Nancy Heiser, what would you do? (2) What do you think would be the possible outcome from that action or actions? (3) Would any risks involved be worth it? Share and discuss these suggestions. It is important to keep a balance between any actions proposed for Nancy or Katy and the need for Linda to examine alternatives and make her own decision. Remember: No one should assume responsibility for Linda's choice and its consequences, because that is the nature of human freedom.

Dr. Weeks sometimes introduces two questions which focus on other issues. He asks if Paul's language about glorifying God in your body (1 Cor. 6:19-20) applies to this case? How? In what ways? Also, how does it relate to Paul's concern that Christians are free for all things but responsible for not causing a brother to stumble (Rom. 14:21; 1 Cor. 8:9)?

Raise the question of *why* persons turn to the use of drugs. Make a list of suggestions that are given. Once completed, discuss the list. Attention can also be given to the following suggestions from John King:

1. Low self-esteem, self-awareness.
2. Lack of coping skills for stresses which threaten sense of well-being.
3. Unclear sense of values.
4. Cannot communicate thinking, feelings, or longings to others.
5. Difficulty in relating to others.
6. Means to defy authority.
7. Boredom coupled with availability of drugs where persons have no constructive, wholesome use of time.[7]

The positive side of this case is the issue of long-range factors within families which may help to prevent use of drugs. Lead the group to list some family factors which can help *prevent* youth from turning to drugs. Now examine the following suggestions for their value for such prevention.

1. Love and affection from family members.
2. An environment as free as possible from sarcasm and hostile criticism.
3. Parents who meet crises and stress without using alcohol or other drugs.
4. Honest, accurate answers to questions about sex, drugs, religion, and the meaning of life.
5. Family relationships that permit expressions of feelings and thoughts and adequate time for listening creatively to each other.
6. Help if one is experiencing anger, grief, or disappointment.
7. A vital religious faith in God and regular participation in church life so that lasting values may be developed.[8]

This case could bridge over into a later study of drugs, parent-youth relations, and other possibilities. In any event, the discussion may conclude with the sharing of some "reflections" group members want to make about the entire incident.

Suggested Resources

Brook, Judith S., and Lettier, Dave J., *et. al. Alcohol and Substance Abuse in Adolescence.* New York: Haworth Press, 1985.

Campbell, Ross. "Ministry in a Chemical Crisis." Ross, Richard, and Hayes, Judi, comps. *Ministry with Youth in Crisis.* Nashville: Convention Press. 1988.

Ross, Richard, comp. *The 24-Hour Counselor*, 2 sets. Nashville: Broadman Press. 1989.

Rowatt, G. Wade. "Substance Abuse." *Pastoral Care with Adolescents in Crisis.* Louisville, Ky.: Westminster/John Knox Press. 1989.

Smith, Gean D. "Substance Abuse: Parents Beware." *Living with Teenagers*, July-September 1983, 40-43.

Uslander, Arlene S. "What Every Parent Should Know About Drug and Alcohol Abuse." *Living with Teenagers*, October-December 1980, 19-20.

8

The Prayer Club

Alex Benson was walking through the crowded high school hallway on his way to class when he saw Susan Dean coming in his direction.[1] She waved and squeezed through the crowd toward him.

"I need to talk to you," she said as they moved toward the wall to get out of the traffic. Susan was a casual acquaintance; Alex knew her mainly through their mutual participation in the school's prayer club. Alex thought he knew why she looked so concerned.

"Tim is pretty upset over what you did in the prayer club meeting yesterday morning," Susan began. "He says he'll never come back, and I can't really say that I blame him."

Alex started to interrupt, but she quickly continued: "You didn't let him speak. You especially invited him to that meeting to present his viewpoint, and you didn't even give him a chance to say anything. He and his friends thought he would be able to explain their views and you just ignored them. You really insulted them, and I think it's awful." Before he could answer, she briskly walked away.

Susan's emotional accusation surprised Alex. He felt she had a point, but until now he had not fully begun to realize the extent of the problem which had developed.

Alex Benson and the Prayer Club

Central High School was five years old and had approximately 800 students. It was one of several high schools located in a densely populated, industrial county in eastern Tennessee. The school's prayer club had been in existence since shortly after the school opened and was presently sponsored and advised by two faculty members—Mrs. Kennedy, an English teacher, and Mrs. LaSalle, one of the school's guidance counselors. During the school's first four years, the prayer club averaged fifteen to twenty members. However, during the previous summer a strong religious revival had an impact on eastern Tennessee and many of Central's young people. When school opened in the fall, forty students were at the club's first meeting.

Alex Benson was a senior and president of the prayer club. He was a quiet, almost shy young man, but confident when it came to religious matters. He had been elected president at the end of the last school year and now found himself responsible for leading a much larger group than he had anticipated. He was liked and respected by members of the club and had a good relationship with the faculty advisers, particularly Mrs. LaSalle. He often talked with her about his college and vocational plans, as well as plans for the prayer club. Alex was an active member of his church.

After the club's first meeting of the school year, Alex felt he could recognize that there were three distinct groups with which he would have to be concerned. One was the group of *old members*—young people who had previously been actively involved in local, rather conservative (theologically and politically) churches almost all their lives. Another group, and the largest of the three, was the *new members.* This group included young people with diverse religious backgrounds and personalities, who were similar in that each professed to having had a recent, life-changing spiritual experience.

Also, members of this second group were strongly attracted to a third group whose members called themselves *charismatics.* These youth, who were not usually involved with the prayer club, had what the new converts saw as a very exciting type of religion. Their being "filled with the Spirit" was verified, they claimed, through their possession of the "gift" of healing and especially the "gift" of being able to "speak in tongues." They held this latter gift to be promised by the Bible as a "second blessing" for true believers in Christ, citing Acts 2:4f; 8:17; 9:17.

Alex and the old members of the club were concerned that some of the new converts, who were beginning to believe that speaking in tongues was an absolutely necessary sign that one was "Spirit-filled" and perhaps even a test of true Christian salvation, were confused and anxious because they had not yet experienced "the gift." Therefore, Alex and the other club officers decided to have a discussion in one of their meetings about speaking in tongues. They believed it might help reassure the newer members about their faith as well as improve communication between the prayer club and the charismatics. Alex also decided to invite Tim Martin to the meeting to represent the viewpoint of one who had actually spoken in tongues. Mrs. LaSalle advised Alex not to have that type of meeting, but he thought she was being overly cautious and proceeded with plans for it.

The Charismatics

There were seven or eight young people in the school who were members of a local church known for speaking in tongues. Though she did not claim to have spoken in tongues, Susan Dean was the only one of this group who was also a member of the prayer club. It was through her that Alex met Tim Martin, invited him to attend the meeting, and join in the discussion. Tim's father was pastor of the church that the charismatics attended, and Tim was their "leader" at school. He was a quiet, unimposing person but confident about his religious practices and the biblical basis for his beliefs. He was impressed that Alex would invite him to participate at a prayer club meeting, and he gladly accepted the invitation.

Preparing for the Meeting

The night before the meeting Alex stayed up rather late studying Scripture references on the subject of gifts and tongue-speaking and thinking about how would be best to conduct the meeting. He gave particular attention to Romans 12:3-8; 1 Corinthians 12:8-10, 28; Ephesians 4:1ff, and verses surrounding each passage. He knew that it would be easy for emotions and personalities to become involved and could be damaging to the club and everyone concerned. He was convinced he would need to be fair and careful in the way he presided.

The Meeting

About fifty people crowded into the classroom for the meeting. There were two college students in the back of the room who were members of a nondenominational church in which three of the new club members had become involved. Alex had met them before, but they had been invited to the meeting without his knowledge. Tim Martin and his friends sat at the front of the room. Mrs. Kennedy and Mrs. LaSalle were not present, though Alex had asked them to attend.

Alex was nervous but optimistic. He greeted the group, led in prayer, made a few remarks about the purpose of the meeting, and declared the floor open for the discussion. He had decided to recognize the first hand raised each time a question was asked in order to keep himself from intentionally playing favorites.

There were some strong feelings about this subject. One student wanted to know what speaking in tongues was and another replied, "It's the baptism of the Holy Spirit of God. You just turn yourself over to the Holy Spirit. Paul talks about it in 1 Corinthians 12."

Another student asked, "What caused speaking in tongues?"

A student who professed to having had the experience explained that it "just comes over you when you try to pray, and the Holy Spirit speaks through you. You don't know what you're saying because it's the Holy Spirit speaking. It just makes sounds through you."

Still another student wondered what it really signified. "What value or good is it?" she said. She was told it is when you really feel close to God and turn your life over to Him fully. God uses you to speak His words.

Alex was uncomfortable with the presence and comments of the two college students who spoke authoritatively against the importance of speaking in tongues. They cited 1 Corinthians 13 and 14 as the basis for their views and seemed to be attempting to win an argument rather than participating in a discussion.

The discussion was still "going strong" when the bell rang for morning classes to begin. Thinking the meeting had gone smoothly, Alex made a closing comment and concluded with prayer. As he looked up he saw Tim closing his Bible with some force and, with a seeming look of disgust, walk quickly from the room. Susan gave Alex an angry look and followed Tim. Alex suddenly realized he had not once recognized Tim because he had never been first to raise his hand. He *had* raised his hand several times, but apparently because he sat in the front of the room Tim was unaware of all the competition to speak from those behind him. Alex, in his effort "to be fair to everyone" and in his nervous lack of attention, had not specifically called on Tim to speak.

Reflections on the Meeting

As Susan disappeared in the crowded hallway, Alex grew gravely concerned about what was happening to the club. He wondered if he had totally alienated Tim and his friends. Did they think his invitation was a trick to get them to the meeting so their viewpoint could be "out-argued"—and perhaps they could be humiliated? Had the discussion fairly presented Tim's viewpoint? How did the meeting reflect on Alex and the whole prayer club? Had the whole thing made the new converts more confused than before? Had it disillusioned them?

Alex had announced that the discussion would probably be continued at the next meeting.

Ponderings for Pedagogy

As Paul wrote: "It is important, fellow Christians, that you should have clear knowledge on the subject of spiritual gifts" (1 Cor. 12:1, author). Of fundamental importance in studying this case is the discussion leader's objective and fair presentation of the side calling itself the charismatics. Such balance may require reading some literature representing this viewpoint. A good source is J. M. Ford's *The Pentecostal Experience* which traces and examines the appearance of charismatics within Roman Catholicism. Wise use could also be made of the experiences of group members and/or their friends who claim the gift of tongues, or to invite a minister or lay person who can represent that viewpoint to participate in the discussion. Other good texts on the Holy Spirit include J. W. MacGorman's *The Gifts of the Spirit,* Frank Stagg's *The Holy Spirit Today,* Dale Moody's *Spirit of the Living God,* and *Spiritual Gifts and the Church* by Donald Bridge and David Phypers. "Speaking in Tongues" is a cassette tape by J. A. Millikin published by Broadman Press which can prove helpful information.

The group discussion should cause members to examine carefully the biblical material in Romans 12; 1 Corinthians 12—14; Ephesians 4; and 1 Peter 4:10-11. The following spiritual gifts are included in these passages without priority being assigned to any: Romans 12:3-8—prophecy, ministrations, teacher, exhortation (encouraging), giving, ruler (leadership), mercy; 1 Corinthians 12:8-10—utterance of wisdom, utterance of knowledge, faith, healing, miracles, prophecy, discernment of spirits, interpretation of tongues; Ephesians 4:11—apostles, prophets, evangelists, pastor-teachers; 1 Corinthians 13—tongues, prophecy, understanding mysteries and knowledge, faith, hope, love; 1 Corinthians 14—unknown tongues, prophecy; and 1 Peter 4:10-11 which addresses the uses for which spiritual gifts are given to the church.

It is important to recognize the tendency to ignore so many of the other spiritual gifts in favor of an inordinate emphasis on tongue speaking and faith healing. Compare tongue-speaking, for example, with the importance of showing mercy, having faith, healing, the ministry of serving, governing, giving, and so forth. Further, labeling those who practice tongue-speaking as "the charismatics" is a misnomer, since the word *charismata* refers to gifts ("things freely given"), not solely or primarily to tongue-speaking. All gifts mentioned in the Bible are *charismatic gifts.* Further, the more than twenty gifts specifically named in Scripture probably do not include all gifts of the Spirit which were known within the early church.

> Were there only one order of workers, what helpful purpose could they serve? Let there be among the Corinthian Christians, and in every Christian church in any age, clear recognition of the simple truth that in such a divinely appointed organism as the body of Christ, for its vitality and its effective witness, a wide variety of functions is required.[2]

It may also be noticed that tongue speaking appears to be the phenomenon which elicits most of Paul's warnings and criticism.

The discussion of this case should serve at least three purposes. It should enlarge a person's understanding of spiritual gifts which are given to Christians by God for use in ministry through His church. Also, it should lead discussants to examine and evaluate the total and broad range of spiritual gifts in the Bible. A final purpose is to aid discussants to "name" their own gifts and to become responsible for the development and use of those gifts.

The "Prayer Club" case study will be useful for youth Bible studies, retreats, workshops on discovering one's gifts, strategies for conflict management, as well as to study leadership, the planning process, or to consider the importance of relationships within a group. Obviously, it can also be used as a vehicle to study tongue speaking. However, the suggestions which follow are designed to use the case as a means for leading youth to confront and deal with religious viewpoints which are different from and may even be in conflict with their own Christian faith rather than to focus solely on speaking in tongues.

Group Leadership

Any human situation involves four factors in some kind of mixture. If the "mix" is adequately balanced and the factors are complementary, harmony and productivity result. If not, there is reason for asking what and how changes need to be made.

Therefore, consider beginning discussion of this case by asking discussants to examine it in terms of these four factors: *task, organization, people,* and *environment.* The items under each word in the following chart illustrate some of the kinds of ideas which may be supplied by participants who should be led to *develop their own lists.*

Task	*Organization*	*People*	*Environment*
Unclear?	Student club	Alex Benson	School
Fellowship?	President	Susan Dean	50 people
Discussion?	Faculty advisers	Tim Martin	Classroom
Prayer?		Mrs. Kennedy	the place for
Set programs?		College students	this discussion?
Agendas?		3 student groups	Advisers?
			Argument?
			Debate?

What do we know about each person? What views do they hold? How is each one involved in the events?

Give attention to the reasons why Alex and the club officers (are there any others?) originally scheduled the meeting. Possibilities include: to reassure new Christians about their faith, improve communications between Prayer Club and charismatics, appease Susan, "show" the advisers, and "show up" the charismatics. Encourage suggestions by the group.

Lead the group to examine the factors affecting the outcomes of this meeting. One effective way is to use a form of "force field analysis" (developed by Kurt Lewin) and ask group members to assign each factor they identify a positive or negative value for achieving the purposes of the meeting. Divide a sheet of paper (this can be done by each individual), part of a chalkboard, newsprint, or poster board with a vertical line, placing a plus over the left section and a minus over the right. Write *10* at the top of the vertical line. Place a zero an equal distance from the right and left. Now ask group members to identify plus and minus factors and place a dot on the chart according to the group''s perception of the impact of each factor (plus or minus *and* strength 0 to 10) on the meeting. Let group members discuss why they made their choices.

Ask participants to identify issues they see involved in this case. Other study groups have identified: Alex versus Mrs. LaSalle's advice, treatment of Tim Martin, tongue speaking, biblical interpretation, and unclear goals.

Biblical Resources

In order to give attention to the biblical material divide the group into as many as five groups (depending on total group size) and assign each group one or more of the biblical passages listed earlier under "Ponderings for Pedagogy." Allow time for them to consider the significance of their passage(s) for the prayer club, with their conclusions to be reported later to the larger group.

Follow the group reports and discussion by pointing out the role of gifts in the doctrine of the laity as it is reflected in 1 Corinthians 12. The following is an outline which can help to guide this Bible study.

Spiritual Gifts in 1 Corinthians 12
1. Different Gifts: Varieties (v.4). The same Spirit
   Service (v.5). The same Lord
   Working (v.6). The same God
2. Each Christian has a spiritual gift(s) (v.7).
3. Gifts exist for the "common good" (v.7).
4. Gifts belong to the body of Christ, His church . . . so things may be done "decently and in order."
5. Gifts must be used for their intended purposes.

What About a Role-Play?

Consider choosing two persons to role play a discussion in which Alex has asked to talk with school counselor Mrs. LaSalle in her office.

If feasible, the following information about each character is suggested to be supplied separately without the knowledge of the other player.

Role-Play—The Prayer Club

Mrs. LaSalle

Assume that Alex Benson has made an appointment to see you. Acting as a school guidance counselor, welcome him into your office and have a conference with him about his concerns.
Considerations:

1. You assume he has come to talk about the next meeting of the prayer club.
2. You have heard about the club meeting.
3. Remember that you *advised* Alex against scheduling the meeting.
4. What kind of problems were created by the meeting?
5. What and how will you advise Alex to proceed with the club?

Alex Benson

Assume that you are Alex Benson. You have made an appointment to see Mrs. LaSalle, the school guidance counselor, who is your friend. You are welcomed into her office.
Considerations:

1. Mrs. LaSalle assumes you want to talk about the meeting of the prayer club. Do you?
2. Begin with some questions or comments about your college plans for the fall. Remember that you have talked some with her about this before.
3. When you want, move into a discussion regarding the previous meeting and next meeting of the prayer club.
4. Be *firm* about the "rightness" of your original decision to schedule the meeting around the topic of speaking in tongues, even if she did advise against it.
5. Press Mrs. LaSalle for some specific guidance and help. Remember that neither she nor Mrs. Kennedy bothered to attend your meeting.

Following the role play, raise this possibility: If Alex came to you as his friend and asked your counsel, what would you advise him to do next? List all suggestions and then see if there is any group consensus about the preferred one(s). Consideration may be given to "what might happen" if each suggestion were implemented.

Particularly if *youth* are discussing the case, rather than finally focusing only on tongue speaking, lead them to think about how Christians can dialogue with and witness to persons who hold religious beliefs which differ from their own. Bryant Hicks, who has served as a youth minister, pastor, foreign missionary, and professor gives these suggestions.

• Begin by clarifying where you are in your own faith and beliefs. Know where you stand in your faith and its biblical basis.

• Know or learn as much as is feasible about the other person's beliefs and religion, recognizing you are relating primarily to a *person* rather than a religion—to a *person* of another system of religious beliefs.

• Be affirming, appreciative, accepting, and positive toward this *person.* Avoid trying to tear down and alienate either by wit, attack, or ridicule.

• Focus primarily on Jesus Christ as a *person.* This was the pattern of Peter, Paul, John, and others in the Bible. Emphasize Christianity as a faith response to Jesus Christ rather than a set of predetermined beliefs to force upon others.

• Actively cultivate them socially and personally. Youth need to see a practical demonstration of Christian behavior in attitude, concern, love, caring, and so forth, if they are to become followers of Christ. Remember that God came *personally* in Christ Jesus.

• Tell forthrightly what Jesus Christ has done and is doing in your life right now.

• Be friendly, warm, caring, and loving. Learn to be an active listener. Remember you have two ears and only one mouth.

• Discuss the authority for faith. Ask, On what do you base your faith? Have them to declare themselves. You must be prepared to share that your authority is Jesus Christ and the Bible.

• Avoid "agreement" with another view. Instead, focus on giving personal testimony rather than debating an issue.

• Pray with the person and for the person in his or her presence, thanking God for forgiveness, salvation, and the joy you feel.

• Seek counsel and aid of other Christians in whom you have confidence. You may want to invite another Christian to join you in talking with the person. It is no accident that groups with strong witnessing emphases almost always send persons out to witness by twos—just as Jesus did. See Matthew 4:18, 21; 11:2; 21:1; Mark 6:7; 11:1; 14:13; Luke 10:1; 19:29; and Acts 19:22.

• Maintain your confidence about your own faith and the future. Plant seeds and trust God for the increase. Maintain your own spiritual vigor. Be genuinely humble but confident about your own faith.

- Do not attack, scorn, or ridicule the group. Be courteous but firm, focusing on the love and grace of God rather than on sin and judgment. Instead of arguing, be a joyful, caring witness for Christ.

Suggested Resources

Braswell, George W., Jr. *Understanding Sectarian Groups in America.* Nashville: Broadman Press, 1986.

Igleheart, Glenn A. *Church Members and Nontraditional Religious Groups.* Nashville: Broadman Press, 1985.

Martin, Walter. *The Kingdom of the Cults.* Minneapolis: Bethany Fellowship, 1968.

McBeth, Leon. *Strange New Religions,* rev. ed. Nashville: Broadman Press, 1977.

Perry, Edmund. *The Gospel in Dispute.* Garden City, N.Y.: Doubleday, 1958.

Starkes, M. Thomas. *Confronting Popular Cults.* Nashville: Broadman Press, 1972.

Contact Interfaith Witness Department, Home Mission Board of the Southern Baptist Convention, 1350 Spring Street, NW, Atlanta, GA 30367.

Spiritual Counterfeits Project, P.O. Box 4308, Berkeley, CA 94704. (Extensive materials on cults, sects, and so forth.)

The 24-Hour Counselor tapes, Baptist Sunday School Board, 127 Ninth Avenue North, Nashville, TN 37234. (Two sets: Parents of Youth, Youth Doubt editions.)

9

Rose Okoni

"I've looked everywhere in our neighborhood that I can think of and can't find her. A few of her clothes are gone, along with her suitcase. I am very worried and afraid. I just don't know. . . ." Anna Okoni's voice trailed off as she waited for her husband, John, to reply. She somehow hoped for an answer, but none came.

After several seconds which seemed much longer, John replied softly: "We have tried so hard to be good Christian parents. How could all this have happened to us? What did we do wrong? What will our friends say now? Do you think maybe we have done all we can for Rose? Maybe we have been troubled and embarrassed long enough."

The Okoni Family

John and Anna Okoni were respected residents of Benin City in Nigeria. He was employed in the city transportation department under the Divisional Council, and Anna worked as a trader in a local cloth goods store. By local standards, they were an upper middle-class family. With a population of 60,000, Benin City was a significant business center within Bendel State province.

Rose Okoni, almost eighteen now, was an only child, since her elder brother had died at age two. Rose was dearly loved by her parents and their friends. Being a good student, she was liked and respected by peers and teachers in both school and church. She displayed the genuine type of humility and kindness toward others which characterized both her parents. Others saw Rose as "cooperative" and "helpful."

The Okonis were active members of a congregation of about 900 members and participated in Sunday morning and evening services, Bible study, and other activities. Rose had grown up being part of these religious activities and seemed to enjoy them greatly. Fellow church members rejoiced with her parents when Rose publicly professed her personal faith in Christ and was baptized at age ten.

High School

The Benin Christian School was established by the Benin Baptist Association in 1967 as a means for providing quality education in a Christian context. However, in 1972 all public schools were taken over by the government, and private schools were supervised by a state-appointed overseer. With the approval of the rather benevolent area overseer, the Baptist Association renamed their school "Baptist High School" since its concern was with high school level education. Further, since the school's chief financial support came solely from local churches and tuition charges, the school found it increasingly necessary to broaden and enlarge student enrollment.

Rose continued her education by enrolling at Baptist High School when she became fourteen. Her parents were pleased with this development, even though it meant a fifty mile trip each day. Particularly pleasing to them was the fact that the school had a chaplain and Sunday morning and evening worship services for students, though attendance was not mandatory. Nevertheless, the gradual changes toward ecumenism and nonsectarianism were reflected in the present option given to students to select a religion of their choice. Therefore, it was not surprising that Rose became acquainted with some adherents of traditional African religions, as well as a variety of Christian faiths. Youth of various cultural and economic backgrounds were represented among those enrolled in Baptist High School, and some students had little, if any, personal religious faith or commitment.

Experiences as Resident Student

When Rose began tenth grade her parents wanted to enable her to concentrate more on her studies in order to equip her for taking her college entrance exams on finishing high school. To do this her parents decided Rose should stay in residential facilities at the school, believing she would get the best from the school and be able to concentrate more on her studies. This arrangement meant that as a resident student Rose came home only on weekends and holidays.

Resident housing was dormitory style. Rose was placed with seven other girls in one facility, and to her surprise, none of the other girls was a professing Christian. One in particular, Joyce, seemed to delight in ridiculing and challenging some of Rose's religious beliefs and activities, terming them as nonsense, a waste of time, and silly superstition. In time this began to trouble Rose, and encouraged by her other roommates, she began to raise questions about her own faith and the acceptability of what she had always seen as "Christian behavior." *Is God really there? Is there anything wrong, really, with premarital sex?*

Well, I will find time to discuss all this with my mother one day, Rose thought. In Nigeria, it was expected that a daughter's questions would be handled by the mother rather than the father. Rose delayed asking, however.

A couple of times Rose considered talking about her questions with someone within the high school, perhaps a teacher. However, some teachers were hesitant about declaring any personal faith of their own since the government takeover of Nigerian schools. Certain teachers were known not to be Christians. Therefore, Rose felt hesitant about approaching anyone, including the chaplain, whom she did not feel she knew very well.

The Okonis felt pleased about Baptist High School. While they knew generally about the faculty and resident situation at Baptist High, they were quite confident of their daughter's upbringing and did not want to initiate conversation or questions with her about her faith. They felt everything was all right with Rose and were reassured by her enthusiastic attendance with them at worship services when she was home.

Rose's Questioning

During a visit at home, Rose, adopting a joking tone, asked: "Mother, what is really wrong with drinking and smoking? I am just not so certain anymore."

"Drinking and smoking are bad for your health," replied Mrs. Okoni, without probing anymore why Rose should ask such a question at this stage of her life.

"Then why should the government allow people to make strong drinks and cigarettes if they are bad for people's health?" Rose asked.

"You know, the government can allow people to make something if it yields money, provides jobs, and poses as little danger to health as possible. Of course the government will still point out the effect it has on people's lives," her mother concluded.

Feeling that her mother was uncomfortable, Rose decided not to ask any more questions and moved to other conversation.

Finding herself somewhat concerned by Rose's questions, Mrs. Okoni later mentioned the conversation to her husband. "Anna," he replied, "you know, students are fond of asking questions. Rose will understand things better for herself in the future. Don't worry about it."

Changes in Rose's Behavior

Rose did not ask any other "school" questions, nor did Mrs. Okoni raise any. What the Okonis did not know was that Rose had begun secretly to smoke and drink with her roommates and school friends. She had even done so during her home visits—without her parents' knowledge. In fact, she felt some satisfaction when one roommate named Ayo remarked, "We are glad Rose is giving up and getting over some of her childish beliefs and starting to have some fun out of life." Her roommates laughed. Rose felt approval.

In the following months the Okonis noticed changes in Rose's attitude toward the church and her Christian beliefs. She grew somewhat negative toward Christianity and church attendance, and sometimes refused to obey her parents, a disobedience she had never shown before. Quarrels with her parents became more frequent, and Rose's peers grew increasingly more important than her parents. Anna Okoni grew particularly concerned about Rose's attitudes and beliefs.

Dropout, Pregnancy, Disappearance

By Rose's sixteenth birthday, she had dated several boys and experienced sexual intercourse. On reaching seventeen, she decided to drop out of school, even though it was against her parents' wishes. A short time later the Okonis learned that Rose was pregnant. Their feelings of embarrassment and humiliation were intensified by the fact that Rose said she was uncertain which boyfriend was the father of her child. In Nigerian culture the Okonis, like other parents, would be given much respect and honor if their daughter married through "the normal process."

Discussion and Decision

Rose disappeared. As her parents sat talking, Anna Okoni spoke to her husband: "Should we try to look for her? If we can find her, can we rehabilitate her? Or should we just give up about her? I just don't know anymore. What do you suggest be done?"

Within a few moments the Okonis agreed they would search for Rose. Not wanting to make it a matter of public record, they chose not to call the police or check through the school. Instead, over the next several hours Mrs. Okoni made some discreet telephone calls, one of which finally produced the suggestion from one of Rose's friends that she might be at Rebekah's house. A call to Rebekah's home (along with some coaxing) led to an admission by Rebekah that Rose was there. By now, it was past 11:00 p.m.

As quickly as possible, the Okonis drove to Rebekah's home. Although the ensuing conversation with Rose did not seem to resolve anything, Mr. Okoni finally demanded: "Get your things. You are coming home with your mother and me." Unable to resist this direct personal command from her father, Rose silently obeyed and accompanied them to their home.

After an hour of heated discussion, Rose eventually appeared, at least tentatively, to accept the fact that her parents did want to help her, particularly with the future of her baby. With Anna's gentle persuasion, Rose finally identified the father of her baby, an eighteen-year-old whom the Okonis knew.

The Okonis now faced the question of whether or not to involve the baby's father in Rose's pregnancy. If so, how would they go about it? How would the young man react? What if he denied it? What about his parents' reaction? If it became necessary, would Rose agree to his being pressured into his role as father? What is best for Rose? These were some of the questions which troubled the Okonis as they slipped into bed after Rose retired.

Ponderings for Pedagogy

Problems and needs within a family system have a degree of sameness no matter where the family lives, works, and interacts. Communication, acceptance, love, affection, responsibility, and other needs can create coping crises within the framework of family life in any cultural setting. Some feelings and customs may be different, but the struggle for happiness is universal. Tolstoy reportedly said it this way: "All happy families are alike. Each unhappy family is unhappy in its own way."

This case from a third world country has potential for helping youth and their leaders to examine and compare themselves with the Okoni family. In the process, they may detect similarities and parallels, and perhaps experience reductions in their feelings of superiority or prejudice. The case encourages a feeling of identification "that they are pretty much like us." It is affirmation of Richard Armour's tongue-in-cheek comment that "adolescence has broken out everywhere in an especially virulent form" and "almost every one between twelve and twenty has it bad."[1]

Research Data

The half-million or more pre-teen and teenage mothers reported each year reflect a national epidemic in the United States. Sometimes it is called "babies having babies"; some of these mothers are reported to be no more than ten years old.[2] The United States leads all of the world's developed nations in teen pregnancies, with 96 out of 1,000 girls fifteen to nineteen becoming pregnant, that's over twice that of England's number. Drawing upon numerous sources, the Center of Population Options in Washington, D.C., points to these important facts.

- Twenty-three percent of female high school dropouts are due to pregnancy.

- Of women who become mothers before age twenty, less than 2 percent complete college while 20 percent of those who have children after age twenty-four complete college.
- Teenage fathers are only half as likely to complete college as those in their twenties.
- Teenage mothers have lower status occupations, having about one-half less the income than mothers with first pregnancies in their twenties.
- Sixty-seven percent of families headed by mothers who gave birth as teenagers live below the official poverty level in the U.S. In 1985 about 53 percent of the 15.69 billion dollars spent for AFDC (Aid for Families with Dependent Children) went to families in which the mothers had given birth as a teenager.
- Children of teenage parents are more likely to become teenage parents themselves.[3]

The same Center also provides some disturbing data about the often under reported role of fathers in teenage pregnancies.

- The mean age for first intercourse is 16.3 years for males, 17.4 years for females. A Baltimore study found the mean age for first intercourse among inner-city males was 11.8 years.
- Almost 40 percent of adolescent males reported receiving some form of sex education from parents. However, 68 percent in one study reported it consisted of either nothing or counsel to be careful.
- The first time teenagers have intercourse, 48.9 percent use no method of contraception.
- In 1984 at least 109,264 teenage boys became fathers. Over half (63.3 percent) of eighteen-year-olds who were fathers were not living with their children.
- In 1984 the age of the father was recorded in only 63 percent of births by teenage mothers. In those recorded cases, 70 percent of these fathers were under the age of twenty.[4]

The Christian Life Commission of the Southern Baptist Convention has provided further information on the increase in teenage pregnancies and some resulting problems.

- Of the estimated 3,000 American teenage girls who become pregnant each day, 2,300 are unintentional.
- Only about one-half of teenage mothers begin prenatal care in the first three months of pregnancy. Babies receiving late or no prenatal care are three times more likely to die in the first year of life.
- Twenty percent of all low-birth-weight babies were born to teenage mothers.
- Estimates put teenage abortions as high as 450,000 annually. A survey of forty states and the District of Columbia revealed that 27.5 percent of the abortions were for teenage mothers.[5]

The Kentucky Department for Health Services is one of many state government agencies in the U.S. which seeks to ensure that all pregnant women in their region receive proper prenatal care. This agency reported in 1984 that: (1) approximately 20 percent of stillbirths in Kentucky were to teenage mothers; (2) 9 percent of babies born to these teenagers weighed less than five and one half pounds; (3) babies of mothers under age fifteen are twice as likely to die in the first year as those born to mothers fifteen to nineteen years of age; (4) half of all teen mothers rear their children as single parents (thus esuring almost certain poverty); (5) the suicide rate is seven times higher among pregnant teens; (6) teen mothers are more likely to be child abusers; and (7) teen marriages are two to three times more likely to end in divorce.[6]

In 1983, 47 percent of all teen pregnancies in the U.S. ended in birth, 40 percent in abortion, and 13 percent in miscarriage, according to the Alan Guttmacher Institute, a nonprofit research group.[7]

While this data reflects conditions only in the United States, it does show the growing problems resulting from teen pregnancies. Lillian Rubin, a sociologist and psychologist at the Institute for the Study of Social Change at the University of California at Berkeley, reports that today's teenagers feel they make their own decisions about their sexual behavior. She and other experts in teen behavior believe teenagers feel sex is acceptable as long as pregnancy does not result and a monogamous (however brief) rather than promiscuous relationship exists. Teenagers also report that the chief reason they engage in sex before they personally choose to do so is social and peer pressure. Patrick Welsh, teacher at T. C. Welsh High School in Alexandria, Virginia, reports in his 1985 book, *Tales Out of School,* that teens also cite the inconsistency between the avowed traditional morality and the liberal sexual behavior of parents as an important factor.[8]

Another trend in sexual behavior and health in the U.S. involves the epidemic spread of HPV (Human Papilloma Virus) at a rate of one-half million new cases each year. In addition to the genital warts and lesions caused by this disease, one particular strain of HPV causes cervical cancer. Researchers have found that for the last five years teenagers have been spreading this disease at alarming levels. Some studies show that 30 to 35 percent of sexually active teens have HPV, often without knowing it.[9]

Church leaders need to be aware that church youth attitudes and behaviors are like the sexual mores of other American youth, even when the youth attend church. The 1987 "Teen Sex Survey in the Evangelical Church" produced these findings:

- Forty-three percent have had sexual intercourse by age eighteen.
- One-third do not view sex outside of marriage as a morally unacceptable practice.
- Thirty-seven percent of seventeen-year-olds and 26 percent of sixteen-year-olds had experienced sexual intercourse.

These figures compare with a 1986 Louis Harris and Associates poll which reported that 57 percent of the nation's seventeen-year-olds, 46 percent of sixteen-year-olds, and 29 percent of fifteen-year-olds are sexually active.[10]

Most experts also believe that a marked increase in AIDS (acquired immunodeficiency syndrome) among teens is in America's future. One contributing factor is likely to be that only 345 confirmed cases among teens has been reported as of February 13, 1989, making most teens feel "it can't happen to me." As Mark T., a seventeen-year-old from a middle-class family in Washington, says: "A lot of my friends feel that everybody's using the AIDS thing to scare kids into not having sex. It's not going to work. I don't know of one person my age who's died of AIDS."[11]

These and other findings strongly suggest that sexual activity and its attendant consequences among teens are likely to increase, leaving youth, their parents, and society to cope with the problems of teen parents in poverty, undereducated mothers, single parents, child abuse, and a host of other difficult problems.

Group Leadership

The purposes of this case are to examine the growth and some relational patterns of a youth and her parents within a third world culture, identify and evaluate significant teachable moments and turning points in the life of a family system, and consider possible actions for a particular family in crisis.

Uses

This case has many uses. *Youth* can be led to analyze it in regard to the role of the church in moral issues: youth culture versus parental morality; social pressures to drink, smoke, and be sexually active and perhaps promiscuous; abortion; and evaluation of high school education, unwanted pregnancy, and family conflict. *Parents* will see and feel the anxieties, hopes, discouragements, and feelings of despair which can be part of parenting. They will find this case a helpful vehicle for parent discussion, worship, a seminar, or dialogue perhaps under titles such as: "Why Can't I Understand My Kid(s)?," "Discipline: Old-Fashioned or Unnecessary?," "How Can We Help Our Kids?," "Babies Having Babies," "High School: Education or Endurance," and so forth. Incidentally, experience suggests the wisdom of study or seminar titles which attract attention, and, where possible, pose a question or issue, and are personalized.

Guiding Discussion

Careful study of the case should be coupled with development of a time line of events. Since there are only three major figures, identifying them and the minor characters should prove rather simple. Nevertheless, writing down all that is known about each of the persons, including facts and impressions, will be a valuable preparatory exercise for the discussion leader.

Begin the discussion by asking participants to identify the persons and facts about each and record them on a chalkboard or newsprint. Another way to begin is to ask someone, perhaps a specific person, if you know he or she will not mind, to briefly tell the story of Rose Okoni. Still another way to start is to ask: Where did Anna and John Okoni go wrong as parents? Or, Where did Rose go wrong? What's her problem, anyway? What's wrong with the Okoni family? Be alert to the responses and pursue them, especially when they appear to be substantive.

Another effective technique is to divide into two groups, one to view the case from Rose's perspective and the other from that of the parents. This is especially helpful if the group is composed of both youth and parents. Further, consider asking the youth to be "parents" and vice versa in a type of role reversal. This will help each group better understand the other.

Often how a person *feels* about the facts of experience is more significant than the facts themselves. Ask, How would you describe the *feelings* of each person in the case? Record and discuss the responses, including *why* the persons feel as they do.

Issues

The time span covered by this case provides the possibility for identifying and assessing the importance of many issues both for the development of events and the decision point at which the case arrives. Lead discussants to identify all the issues they see as being involved, *without evaluating* the validity of each.

While group members should be the primary contributors of these issues, the leader will want to have thought through the issues which have occurred to him or her. Some which could be considered are:

● Inadequate communication between parent and child, school and home, church and family, and staff and parents. Any one of these could be examined for its type, importance, and so forth.

- The role of the church. Where is the pastor in all of this? The chaplain? Lay leaders of groups in which Rose was involved?
- Application of the church's theology *(orthodoxy)* to its practical work *(orthopraxy)* with youth. Has the church provided adequate answers to the questions Rose is asking? Do we tend to avoid hard questions in favor of easy answers? If so, what are examples in the case?
- Need of parents for support from church, school, and friends. Parents are often isolated and hurting, because they feel they cannot face the trauma of risking the blame they feel will surely come if neighbors and friends find out.
- Premarital sex. What does the Bible teach about premarital sex? Who determines a person's standards of behavior? God? Parents? Peers? What role should parents and the church take in teaching youth about sex?
- Failure of the Okonis to notice cues from Rose's questions, behavior, smoking, and drinking. Could they not know of her smoking at home? Drinking? Were they afraid to learn what they did not want to know? Were her questions dealt with adequately? Why?
- Role of a Christian school. Exactly what is the role of such schools with regard to student behavior? Are school staff persons obligated to report to parents about the behavior and companions of sons and daughters? Should its curriculum include help on coping with peer pressure and moral temptations? Are counseling resources available?
- Legal. Is the legal drinking age an issue? Who is responsible for reporting violations? Role of the school? Of others?
- Role of the baby's father. Does the father know Rose is pregnant? What are his rights? Obligations? What financial and other resources does he have for helping? Should he be *forced* into his role as father? Why?
- Circumstances of the pregnancy. Is this an unwanted pregnancy? Is it intentional? These are crucial questions. Was it an act of rebellion? Did Rose want to have a baby? Could this baby represent for her something or someone to have and love as her own? Does she believe the baby will be a source of love for her? If so, is she likely to be pleased or disappointed? How does she see this child fitting into her relationship with her parents?
- Need to deal with the future rather than search for someone to blame. Why do you think humans feel compelled to search for someone to blame or credit in so many incidents of life? What is the most urgent need in the Okoni situation right now?

Alternative Actions

The lure of identifying persons involved, judging past actions, blaming persons, and discovering issues can become so engaging that we fail to move to examine action possibilities. One way to avoid this is to enlist or appoint persons to role-play the next morning's conversation between the Okonis and Rose. The discussion could be done only between Anna and Rose. Focus attention on *feelings* and *ideas* of each person about what should be done.

After the role- play, examine some possible actions for Rose. These will depend partially on assumptions which are made by the group. For example, does the father know about the pregnancy? Does Rose want to marry? What feelings do John and Anna have about abortion? About adoption? Rearing the baby themselves? The answers to these questions will affect the feasibility of any options open to Rose.

Guide the group to think of *all* the options open to Rose, including adoption, foster parents, avoiding embarrassment by choosing to move away from her community until the baby is born, abortion, adoption by John and Anna, contacting the parents of the father, contacting the father for a conference, asking for the help of their pastor, seeking legal advice, checking with a doctor, leaving the decision entirely to Rose, having Anna quit work and care for the baby while Rose goes back to school, and so forth.

When all options have been recorded, lead the group to evaluate each one by the following factors: Can it be done? Is it feasible? What might reasonably be expected to happen if that action were taken? What is likely to be the effect of that action upon the two central people in the case, Rose and the baby? Be certain that the rights and future of the child are not overlooked or neglected in the discussion.

Perhaps it would be helpful to ask which is the *best* choice from among those in the list. The group may even be asked to vote by raising their hands, thereby seeing the range and strength of opinions in the group.

Resources of Grace

God's grace is a potential in a number of ways. *Forgiveness* is greatly needed, by the Okonis toward Rose and vice versa. It needs to be verbalized and communicated in both directions. Of course, the Okonis need the grace to forgive and accept the child's father, if he is to become an ally in Rose's future. *Support* for the family could come from their pastor and other church friends, including church youth who could prove to be the greatest support Rose can find.

Are there other girls in Benin's who are in similar circumstances?

Perhaps a few of them could be led to meet, dialogue together, and become a continuing mutual support group? Or perhaps Rose could join an already existing group.

The *Bible* needs to be used to deal with guilt which remains. Jesus' acceptance without reservation of persons who were outcast and deemed to be sinners by others should be emphasized. "This man welcomes sinners and eats with them" (Luke 15:2). The Samaritan woman at the well (John 4), the adulteress about to be stoned (John 3), the good Samaritan (Luke 10:25-37), and the woman whose gift of perfume Jesus made famous (Luke 7:36-50) are examples. Rose and the baby's father must be helped to know and accept the truth that God's grace is "greater than all our sins." There is a famous incident when the theologian Karl Barth was asked by some American seminarians what he had learned about Christianity. He reportedly replied, "Jesus loves me, this I know, for the Bible tells me so." Rose needs to experience that simple truth.

Caring professionals such as doctors, nurses, and social service personnel are resources through which grace may come. Their healing voices, skills, and touch may aid in adjustments for the future. The ministry of grace was consistently voiced to Harvard medical students of an earlier era through an annual lecture by Dean Francis Peabody. He reportedly said: "The secret of caring for the patient is *caring* for the patient."

Looking at Learning

A technique often used by case teachers is to ask the group to summarize their learning from the case. One major finding is that an individual youth is never unique in the problems, troubles, and concerns he or she experiences. This case clearly illustrates similarities between Rose and youth of other cultures. Some of these can be listed. Parents and church leaders will also discover parallels with their own parenting, leadership tasks, and styles. Youth discussants may even feel some reassurance to discover they are not different, the only one with "my problem," or isolated. Best of all, they may be moved to talk about their concerns with their leaders and parents. Some myths about persons in other countries can also be corrected or dispelled. Participation in the case discussion by a person of another culture could certainly enrich group learning, especially someone familiar with Nigerian culture.

Helping Pregnant Teenagers

What can helping persons do to assist teenage parents-to-be, fathers and mothers, to cope with unplanned and unwanted pregnancy? Here are some suggestions.

● Study the nature and extent of the problem, nationally and in your own state.

● Examine your own feelings and biases toward the problem and persons who are part of the statistics.

● Help pregnant teens express and deal with their feelings. Most experience at least five emotions. *Shock* is likely to be the initial feeling. *Denial* may last four to five months, in the hope that "this is not really happening to me." *Fear* of the future, pain, responsibility, and so forth is likely. *Despair,* sometimes leading to thoughts of suicide, is not unusual. *Anger* toward the father who is free of the burden, or even toward the unborn child may result. *Guilt* over the pregnancy and/or disappointing parents and others often haunt the teen mother. Help must be given to enable the pregnant teen to begin *coping* with realities and decisions which must be made.

● Help the pregnant teen to know her options: marriage, keep and rear the child as a single parent, or adoption. Secure and provide information about area maternity homes which can provide support, peer contact, counseling, and prenatal care.

● Do not allow the pregnancy to cloud the fact that the parents are still teenagers. Treat them accordingly, building their hope and self-esteem.

● Help teen fathers. They may find it easier to deny parenthood—permanently. They may have similar feelings as the mothers. Help them confront and know their options, feelings, rights, and responsibilities.

● Help parents of the teens work through their loss of dreams and hopes, injured pride, hurt, or humiliation. Encourage continued and improved communication with children, recognizing that the mother of the mother-to-be is most often caught *between* father and daughter.

● Help the pregnant teen "see, experience, and celebrate the joy of giving and having life through this baby, and support her decision to keep or put the baby up for adoption," social worker Earlene Grise-Owens says. Support her choices rather than making choices for her. However, 1 Corinthians 6:19-20 teaches that through the Holy Spirit our bodies become holy ground. Consult Jeanne Warren Lindsay's book, *Pregnant Too Soon: Adoption / An Option.*[12]

Suggested Resources

Fowler, Paul B. *Abortion: Toward an Evangelical Consensus.* Portland, Oreg.: Multnomah Press, 1987.

Mace, David. R. *Abortion: The Agonizing Decision.* Nashville: Abingdon Press, 1972.

Ross, Richard, and Rowatt, G. Wade, Jr. *Ministry with Youth and Their Parents.* Nashville: Convention Press, 1986.

Ross, Richard, and Hayes, Judi. *Ministry with Youth in Crisis.* Nashville: Convention Press, 1988. (See chapter 5, "Ministry in a Sexual Crisis" by John Howell.)

Rowatt, G. Wade, Jr. *Pastoral Care with Adolescents in Crisis.* Louisville, Ky.: Westminster/John Knox Press, 1989.

Skoglund, Elizabeth. *Can I Talk to You?* Glendale, Calif.: Regal Books, 1977.

Strommen, Merton and A. Irene. *Five Cries of Parents.* San Francisco: Harper and Row, 1985.

Szumski, Bonnie, ed. *Abortion: Opposing Viewpoints.* St. Paul, Minn.: Greenhaven Press, 1986.

Excellent materials and resources on unplanned and unwanted pregnancies are available from the Christian Life Commission of the Southern Baptist Convention, 901 Commerce, Suite 550, Nashville, TN 37203. These materials provide biblical insights and support for a sanctity of life viewpoint. Also, see the graded study series on "Sanctity of Human Life" from the The Sunday School Board of the Southern Baptist Convention, Nashville, Tennessee.

10

The Bake Sale

"Where is David Kolb?" asked Reverend Jerry Powell, the pastor of Whitehall Church.

"He will not be coming to the youth council meetings," replied Donna Wallace who was a youth council member.

"He said he would not be coming back ever again," said John Moore, another member of the council.

Pastor Powell had expected some adverse reaction to his personal decision to halt the youth bake sale to raise money, but he did not anticipate that one of the council members would become so angry and quit coming altogether. This whole matter threatened to destroy the confidence which Jerry felt the youth of the church had begun to develop in him as a leader. It also threatened to increase the animosity between the youth and adults of the church.

Forming the Council[1]

Reverend Powell had served as pastor for about two and one-half years. He was called to Whitehall while a student at the college about fifty miles away. During the first two years of his pastorate he completed his college degree and expressed anticipation of entering seminary after graduation. After graduation he decided that it might be wise to gain additional experience before continuing his education. He expressed this desire to many of the leaders of Whitehall, and they agreed to retain his services as pastor on an "annual call" basis. Since the pulpit committee which originally had recommended Powell to the congregation had expressed a desire that a youth program be developed, he decided this would become his primary goal. One of the ways he hoped to achieve this was by forming a youth council.

In a general meeting of young people on Sunday afternoon, Pastor Powell made the suggestion that a youth council be formed to plan future youth activities in conjunction with the total church program and serve as a "sounding board" for the opinions of youth. The idea was accepted by the young people, and it was decided that the council would be comprised of three youth representatives and one adult sponsor. Powell told the youth he anticipated directing the council through its first year of existence by meeting with its members and adult sponsor on a monthly basis.

Elected to the council were Donna Wallace, a senior at the local high school; John Moore, a junior; Sara Moore; and David Kolb, also a junior. The council agreed to meet on the following Sunday and make plans for the next three months. The general session with the young people ended with the new council members being congratulated by their peers. Since Sara Moore was not at this meeting, the pastor agreed with the other members that he would contact her on Monday to see if she would accept the position as adult sponsor.

Sara Moore came from a Methodist background. She had joined Whitehall, a congregation of about 250 members, which was located in a semirural but growing area of the state, after marrying Terry Moore who had attended Whitehall since childhood. Sara, twenty-four, was a college graduate who taught English and biology in the local high school. When Jerry Powell called on Sara to inform her of the young peoples' desire for her to serve as the adult sponsor, she accepted, saying, "It's about time that we did something for our youth. They have been neglected long enough!"

The First Council Meeting

The following Sunday, after the evening worship service, the youth council met for its first session. Pastor Powell described the purpose of this meeting as "organizational" and expressed the hope that all members of the council would feel free to express their feelings and desires about the youth activities.

David Kolb began a period of discussion by asking, "Do you really expect this thing to work? We have tried before to express our opinions to the adults of this church. Most of them will not listen, and the ones who will are too afraid of certain individuals who run this church to try to do anything about it."

"Do the rest of you feel this way?" Powell questioned.

"Most of us feel like 'second-lass' members of the church," Donna Wallace replied. "Many of us know that if during a business meeting we were to suggest something constructive for the church to do our parents would get on our case when we got home."

"You mean you feel you do not have the right as members of this church to 'speak your mind' in a business session?" Jerry asked.

"Yes," replied John Moore.

"I do not think that you are accurate in your evaluation of the feelings of the adults of this church," Reverend Powell stated. "I know that many of them are more than willing to hear your ideas. I do think that this youth council can work if you are patient and constructive with your actions. Tell me what you would like to do as a youth group."

"We would like to help some of the less fortunate people in our community," David interjected. "A lot of them lack enough clothing and food. The only problem is we don't have the money to handle such a project. Our church does not have money designated for the youth to use on mission action projects."

"How would some of you suggest that we raise this money? What specific project should we undertake once we have gotten the funds?" Powell asked.

"Many of the clubs at school have held car washes and bake sales to raise money," suggested Sara Moore. "We would have no problem getting people to donate cookies and cakes so that the money would become 'clear profit.' "

"This sounds like a good idea," responded the pastor. "I have read in our denominational magazines about suggestions that some of our mission organizations should hold car washes to raise money for the foreign missions offering this year. I do not see the difference between a car wash and a bake sale. Besides, this mission action project is one that will directly help our community."

It was decided that the bake sale should be held on the first Saturday in the next month which left two weeks for planning and promotion. The meeting was adjourned.

The Meeting with Tyson Duncan, Chairman of Deacons

On the following Sunday the chairman of deacons of Whitehall Baptist Church approached Jerry and expressed a desire to speak with him after church about "a very important matter."

Tyson Duncan had been chairman of the deacons for the last twenty-two years, during eighteen of those years he had also served as Sunday School director. Several people of the congregation at Whitehall had expressed to Pastor Powell their mixed emotions about Duncan's dominance of the two most important leadership positions in the church. They often remarked that they regretted the fact that he often did things "his own way without regard for the feelings of some who oppose his direction." After he graduated from college, Tyson initially pursued a career in teaching, but later changed to an occupation of farming and selling dairy feed. Five years ago at age sixty, he retired from his job as a salesman to devote his time to his family and farm. At the meeting with Powell, Tyson quickly came to the point.

"I understand that you planned a bake sale with the young people. Is that right?" Tyson asked.

"Yes, that is true," Jerry replied.

"We agreed with you when you first came here as pastor that if the deacons felt that you were out of line in any of your actions then we would tell you, and you would do the same for us," stated Duncan.

"I remember that," said Jerry.

"Well, this bake sale thing is not our way. I would suggest you try some other plan of action. You must know that we do not hold bake sales to raise money. Whatever we want to do must be paid for by offerings and donations," Duncan demanded.

"It has been suggested by some of our denominational magazines that a bake sale or car wash might be a proper approach to raising money for foreign mission offerings. What is the difference between that suggestion and this plan of action?" Jerry quizzed.

"I don't know, and I don't care!" retorted Duncan. "Our responsibility is to this church, and you know as well as I do that this church will not want our young people holding a bake sale. It cannot happen, and it will not happen!"

"How am I supposed to tell the young people this?" Jerry asked.

"That is your problem. You will have to find a way to work it out," Duncan answered.

Informing the Council Members

That afternoon the pastor called Donna Wallace and broke the news to her that the bake sale would be canceled. He then asked her to call the rest of the council members and inform them so they in turn could call the other young people involved. Donna informed Powell that some of the young people would not be happy over this decision, and especially over the fact they would not be left with options for future fund-raising projects. Powell explained that he knew there would be some anger over the matter, but he felt they had no choice. He also told Donna he hoped the council could meet as soon as possible to make other plans for the next three months. Donna said she felt they should meet on the following Sunday, and perhaps they could explore the possibility of going directly to the church and asking them for money to help the needy of the community. Powell said that might be a possibility, and they would discuss it at the next council meeting.

The Second Council Meeting

It was during this second meeting of the youth council that Powell learned David had told the rest of the members he would not be coming to any more of the meetings. When asked if David had given a reason, the council members simply reported he was not going to attend any more, nor would he help with any activities they might plan. When asked if David's absence had anything to do with the decision to cancel the bake sale, all the council members would say was "I don't know." Jerry then questioned the youth about their personal feelings over the cancellation of the bake sale.

"We tried to tell you that it was useless to plan any activities for the youth," John explained.

"Most of us feel that we should have been asked about the decision," added Donna. "We think that you might have 'sold out' on your commitment to us. We really can see no need to plan activities for the next quarter if everything we plan must be approved by the adults, and you have the power to cancel them at any time."

Powell then told the members of the youth council about his meeting with Tyson Duncan and expressed regret over his own "poor personal judgment." He assured the council that if they wanted to raise money for any project they would now have to do so by love offerings and gifts. He also expressed his disappointment that David had decided to quit the council, promising he would try to contact him and personally apologize for the misunderstanding. The meeting was then adjourned without plans for the next quarter having been made.

The Meeting with Robert Kolb

David's father, Robert Kolb, was a fifty-seven-year-old deacon in Whitehall Church. Born and reared in the Whitehall community, he remained there to engage in a career of farming. Robert was presently married to his second wife, Helen, who was the mother of David and his younger sister Jane. Robert's first wife had died of cancer leaving a third child, Sandy, who was now married and had children of her own. On the Wednesday after the second youth council meeting, Robert saw Jerry in a local store and began to talk with him about David's absence from the youth council meeting.

"I am sorry that David was not there last Sunday night," Robert said. "He came home Sunday from church and said he was never going back again. We have always made the children go to church. However, we couldn't persuade him to go to the council meeting."

"It is quite all right," Jerry responded. "I think I can understand some of David's feelings."

"He sure is mad at you," Robert interjected. "He said you had no right to make the decision to cancel the bake sale alone. He said you were not willing to stand up to Tyson Duncan, and he didn't care what happens now at church."

"Well, I hope we can get things straightened out," Jerry said. "I have to do what is best for the church and at the same time try not to alienate anyone. That's a pretty hard job."

"I wish you a lot of luck," Robert responded. "We have always let

David express his own opinions, and I'm afraid it has made him a bit stubborn. I do wish that you two could settle your differences. I don't want David to have a bad attitude toward church. I think if anyone can work things out you can."

Robert told Jerry that David might be at the high school playing basketball, and that is where Jerry found him about thirty minutes later.

The Meeting with David Kolb

There were nine boys in the gym playing pick-up basketball, and when Powell came in, obviously dressed to play, they invited him to play to make two full teams. After the game was over and some of the other players had left the gym, Powell approached David, who was resting on a bench, and began a conversation.

"I think that we need to talk," Jerry said.

"About what?" David replied sharply.

"Some of the things that have happened in church for the last few weeks . . ." began Powell before being quickly interrupted.

"I don't think there is much to talk about with you," David retorted. "I don't care if you ever get things going with that stupid youth council. I'm not going to help. I told you that this thing would never work."

"Tell me why you are not willing to be patient and see this thing through?" Jerry asked.

"I don't have to tell you. You know why," David replied.

David then walked away.

Ponderings for Pedagogy

No matter of church life is perhaps more potentially controversial than the collecting and spending of money. Strong and emotional feelings often surface when the subject arises. Its emphasis from the pulpit risks the pastor's being charged with "always talking about money." Congregations have become divided over such matters as spending money on new hymnals versus red carpeting, and heated business meetings have resulted from disagreements over staff salaries, mission offerings, the purchase of computers, and auto allowances for the staff.

Youth are sometimes caught in these disagreements among adults about church financing. The chief reason is that youth are almost totally dependent on adults for financing most of their programs. Even youth fund-raising efforts are ultimately dependent on getting adults to contribute or buy whatever is being sold. Of potentially greater significance is the fact that the financial support of adults often is a barometer of adult perceptions of the role and function of youth within the church congregation.

This is well illustrated in an old saying that "children are the church of day after tomorrow and youth are the church of tomorrow." Whether intended or not, the obvious conclusion then is that "adults are the church of today," not children or youth. Nowhere is this philosophy clearer than in the way adults participate in funding youth ministry. Will it be paternalism or genuine inclusion, conditional handouts or enthusiastic support?

The case illustrates these and other aspects of the nature of youth ministry in a local church. As the family of God, the church must integrate and empower all participants in its life, giving everyone opportunity to *be* the church in a variety of ways. Unobstructed participation in church organizations and leadership, coupled with the intentional distribution of the right to self-direction must become part of that integration and empowerment. Neither money, position, "nor any other creature" can be allowed to prevent it. The basic issue is therefore whether youth will be full members of the church—"young laity" Sara Little called them—or merely communicants *with* the adult church.

One clue as to why asking people to contribute their money to a cause or group can be a sensitive issue may lie in the record of giving habits. Jane Bryant Quinn of *The Washington Post* points out some interesting facts about the giving of Americans.[2] She affirms that the traditional ideal for religious persons is the tithe or 10 percent. However, she reported that a commissioned Gallup Poll found it is a rare family that gives 10 percent to *anything*. Therefore, charities are now proposing a standard for Americans called the "Give Five," meaning 5 percent of income to charity, a goal which acknowledges the fact that in 1987 only 9 percent of America's households gave 5 percent or more. In fact, one-third gave less than one percent and nearly 29 percent gave nothing.

Quinn reports that Protestant giving has continued to decline (3 percent to 2.8 percent between 1968-85) as did Roman Catholic contributions (3.4 percent to 1.4 percent between 1963-84).

Perhaps the most surprising statistics from the Gallup study she cites include:

- Households with under $10,000 income give an average of 2.8 percent to charity.
- Incomes $75,000 to $100,000 gave 1.7 percent.
- $100,000 to $200,000 gave 2.1 percent.[3]

Most Americans give to charity because it is tax-deductible. What are other motives? Philip Yancey says giving can be polluted by any undermining of the *recipient's* dignity. He has sought to recover the true and good meaning, therefore, of words like *pity* (from *piety*), *chari-ty* (*agape* in 1 Cor. 13, KJV), *patronizing* (from *patron*), *paternalism* (from *pater* or *Father*), and *condescend* (seen in Jesus' example as described in Phil. 2:5-7). Yancey asks: Can we reclaim these words and their true meaning through our giving which is motivated by *love*?[4]

Of seventeen denominations whose 1984 giving records were reported by the Research Division of the Home Mission Board of the Southern Baptist Convention, the Christian Missionary Alliance ranked first with $978.50 per capita giving while Southern Baptists were fifteenth with $255.37 per capita.[5] There is growing concern that the recent upward trend in America's overall charitable giving is declining.[6]

What thoughts, questions, or ideas do these facts create for your thinking about charitable giving and worthy projects—be it public or church giving? This data should be helpful preparation for thinking about budgets and fund-raising at Whitehall Church.

Themes

The title and content of this case make funding of the youth project a natural theme. How can the youth council fund its project for the needy of their community? What is the proper role of Pastor Powell and the adult leaders in this effort?

Nevertheless, an even more important theme may be the relationship of youth to the adults in Whitehall Church. It appears to be a troubled relationship which is in danger of further deterioration. The feelings of the youth about adult control of the church do not generate excitement among youth to participate or to reach out to other youth. This underlines the theme of fair representation in decision making, especially in those decisions which directly affect the youth program.

The youth council demonstrates the themes of caring and loving others whom youth see as disadvantaged. They want to act on their compassion for "the least of these" by doing good, to concretize ministry and allow the Word to become flesh in themselves.

Other themes could include the role of a youth council, adequacy of pastoral leadership, courage to do what is unpopular, and the mission vis-à-vis the maintenance dimension of church life.

Uses

This case is ideally suited for use in a parent-youth dialogue since it permits consideration of many aspects of their relationships—in church and at home. The same can be said for its use in studying the basic nature of the church because it is an excellent vehicle for identifying aspects of the church such as acceptance, ministry, community, and mutual respect. It can also serve as an introduction to a series of sermons on the nature and mission of the church.

Youth leaders have also found this case to be an aid in examining a philosophy of youth ministry. What is the nature of an adequate youth ministry in a church? What goals are legitimate for that concept? Youth can react to the events of this case, pointing out what they view as unsatisfactory in the situation and thereby express their views about youth and the church. However, care should be taken to avoid emphasizing only the negative factors and thereby allowing the group to merely engage in an unconstructive gripe session.

Retreats, Bible studies, camps, training events, and conferences involving youth are excellent settings for using this case study. It can serve as either a vehicle to introduce a larger event or as a study within itself.

Group Leadership

Ask the group to name and briefly identify the seven people in this case. Since preparation for leading the discussion should involve constructing a "time line" for the events, the group may also find value in constructing an overall picture for the sequence of events, recorded on the chalkboard, if possible. This should not become too time consuming since dealing with other matters is more important.

This case is not the only one in this book which makes evident the dilemma faced by a case teacher, namely, how much structure to preplan and bring to the discussion. Some teachers feel it should just happen, having the leader "go with the flow" of the group discussion, while others want a more planned session. Much experience and observation demonstrates that every case leader has a framework for their discussion—even if the choice is none at all!

The best case teachers guide discussion around certain key points and skillfully frame their questions. Consider the degree of control you want to exercise in leading the study of this case and then build a teaching plan which may be enriched by some ideas which are reflected in the following outline.

(1) How would you describe the relationship between youth and adults at Whitehall? Why do you feel it is that way? Specific evidence?

(2) What do you think are the views or perceptions of the church held by the youth? Reverend Powell? Sara Moore? David Kolb? Donna Wallace?

(3) How are the church youth viewed by the pastor? Tyson Duncan? Robert Kolb? Sara Moore?

(4) What do you feel are the *real issues* involved in the case? Some

which have been suggested developed by other groups may be examined.

- Relationship of youth to their church and *the* church.
- Self-determination by youth.
- Traditional views of "the Baptist way" versus human needs.
- Tyson Duncan's multiple roles in the church.
- Relationship of youth and adults.
- Pastor's relationship to youth: levels of confidence, integrity, courage.
- Power of the pastor, youth, and Tyson Duncan? Is there competition?
- Ways to secure adequate support for youth programs.

(5) How do you feel Jerry Powell has handled matters?

- Classify his leadership style:
Democratic, autocratic, paternal, laissez-faire, situational, status?
- Powell's view of leadership is:
Negotiator, survivor, coach, joker, benevolent, autocrat, martyr, healer, what?
- How do you feel the pastor handled the cancellation by Tyson Duncan?
- How do you feel about his relationship and leadership with the youth council?

(6) What questions or "whys" remain in your mind about the way Pastor Powell has handled the situation? Any mistakes? Here are a few ideas which have been considered by other groups:

- Did he not know the church well enough by now to ask questions before letting the youth get this far?
- Why did he wait so long before going to see David Kolb?
- Why did he call Donna Wallace and leave it to her to contact the other youth council members? Copout?
- Should he simply accept Tyson Duncan's views and ultimatum? Why?
- Why didn't he try to receive some of Tyson Duncan's affirmative "plan of action?"

(7) Is there still room for renegotiation? Ask the group what youth *said* during the second council meeting, insisting they identify the words ("useless to plan any activities for youth" and so forth). Further, ask about the words of Donna Wallace and Robert Kolb in reacting to the cancellation. Does all this suggest there may still be room to renegotiate? Why?

(8) Let's think about what Reverend Powell can do at this point. What are his options? Here are some suggested by other discussants:

- Forget David Kolb. Work with other youth.
- Go back and replan with the youth council.
- Take the request of the youth council to the church congregation. Confront and answer the questions, including those of Tyson Duncan.
- Go to the congregation with two proposals:
Approval of the project for the needy.
Approval of the financing plan. (Emphasize and sell the *project* rather than the funding.)
- Go to the entire group of deacons with the project. Have they made a decision or is the cancellation the sole idea of Tyson Duncan? Would Tyson act differently in the context of all the deacons including Robert Kolb?
- Talk to Tyson about *his ideas* for acceptable fund raisers. Once he suggests agreeable options, invite him to make the first gift.

While there are immediate action options for the pastor, if he plans to remain as the church leader, what are some *long-range actions* he ought to consider? Youth may suggest a number of constructive possibilities. Among these are resources for grace available through prayer, Bible study, open dialogue, forgiveness, reconciliation with the youth, inclusion of parents, and other caring adults in the church.

A concluding activity can be to analyze what can be *learned* from the Whitehall Church about true Christian fellowship, mission, persons versus programs, reconciliation, and the role of youth in the church.

Another result of using this case has been discussion of *guidelines* for acceptable fund raising projects by the group. Helpful ideas from the group can be linked to their suggestions about specific projects they would like to undertake which meet their own guidelines.

Suggested Resources

Mickey, Paul A., and Wilson, Robert L. *Conflict and Resolution.* Nashville: Abingdon Press, 1973.

McSwain, Larry, and Treadwell, William. *Conflict Ministry in the Church.* Nashville: Broadman Press, 1981.

Lewis, G. Douglass. *Resolving Church Conflicts.* San Francisco: Harper and Row, 1981.

Filley, Alan C. *Interpersonal Conflict Resolution.* Glenview, Ill.: Scott, Foresman and Co., 1975.

11

Lockin

"Have you seen the guy wearing the red shirt?" Beverly inquired anxiously of Mary.

"No, I saw him before the movie started, but I don't see him now." Quick glances around the room revealed that Tommy was indeed missing, as well as several other youth.

"Where could they be?" Mary asked, as they hurriedly began to search. Jack returned in a short while only to relate that they could not be found anywhere within the church building.

First Church Lockin[1]

Mary Cauthen, part-time minister of youth at First Church, had been making plans for over a month for a lockin for the senior high youth group. It had been scheduled to be held at the church on a Friday night after a home football game. Many youth seemed anxious to come and bring friends to share in this time of all-night activities which would conclude with breakfast on Saturday morning.

The pastor had been explicit in making sure that Mary understood that adult members of the church must be present to help supervise the activities and see that nothing went wrong to cause the church any embarrassment. Also, he had clearly emphasized that a detailed program was essential to the effectiveness of the lockin. The pastor had checked Mary's plans for activities to be sure they were appropriate and was anxious to ensure a program's success through proper planning.

Mary, a seminary student, had come to the church as a full-time summer staff worker, but the pastor felt it necessary to ask her to continue working with the youth in the fall on a part-time basis until other arrangements for a full-time worker could be made.

Lockin Schedule

Though she had attended several lockins, this would be Mary's first time to lead one, and she wanted it to be an event the youth would enjoy. She had outlined a flexible schedule to be sure the whole program would progress from one activity to another in ways which would keep the youth interested and involved. The "working schedule" she had designed was as follows:

Friday
10:30 p.m.—Gathering of participants. Table games available. Time for informal visiting activities. Everyone stays in the same room.
11:00—Doors locked; have orientation to program. Announce guidelines and go over evening schedule that is posted in appropriate areas of church.
11:15—"Getting to Know Someone," several exercises to help youth get acquainted with each other. Announce "Air Band Competition" later. Explain how it will be done.
11:45—Snacks, refreshments, and general activities.

Saturday
12:30 a.m.—"Growing Up Toward Each Other," using Ephesians 3:14-21. Discuss boy-girl relationships.
12:50—"Ghost Run," preplanned scavenger hunt through building in which groups look for hidden notes. Counselors stationed to supervise. Prizes given to top three finishers.
2:00—Free time. "NFL Bloopers" movie shown. Refreshments. Group games to be available.
4:00—"Air Band and Lip-sync Competition." Give prizes for different categories.
4:45—Distribute upcoming schedule of youth activities. Discuss future events.
5:00—Devotional Bible study, "Responsibility for Taking a Christian Stand," based on Tony Campolo's, "You Can Make a Difference."
5:30—"Sit Down Volleyball" game.
6:15—Begin preparation for breakfast.
6:35—Serve breakfast of cereal, bacon, eggs, toast, milk, orange juice, and coffee.
7:00—Begin to clean up all areas of church used by youth.
7:30—Close in prayer circle.
7:45—Depart for home.

Enlisting Adult Leaders

The recruitment of adult chaperons presented a problem because many who worked well with the youth were not available for that particular Friday night. Mary was trying to avoid using parents if at all possible, feeling that the presence of parents could create an awkward situation for their children. Finally, three adults agreed to attend and help: Jack Hunter, part-time minister of education and father of one of the boys attending; Beverly Snyder, mother of a senior high girl who would not be attending; and Donna Owens, a new Sunday School teacher for the senior high girls who was anxious to get to know the girls better.

The Lockin

The lockin was to be held in the church's large lower auditorium which had kitchen facilities, rest rooms, and, of special importance, all doors could be locked in the area. However, one door in this area led outside to a parking lot. Though locked from the outside, this door could be opened from the inside.

By 11:00 p.m. nearly thirty-five youth, almost a quarter of whom were visitors, were locked-in as Mary gathered the group together to establish some ground rules and introduce visiting youth, adult leaders, and two other friends of Mary who were to lead in the group singing. Her two friends had already been leading in some informal activities as the youth were arriving. The most specific rules Mary announced included sleeping when desired, no closed doors to anterooms, and if anyone left the building through the door leading outside or caused any unnecessary trouble, parents were to be called and the person(s) would be sent home.

The first part of the experience seemed to be progressing rather well when Joyce, one of the visitors, asked Mary, "Is it OK to smoke?"

When Mary explained that no smoking was allowed in the church building, Joyce questioned further, "Can we go outside to smoke?" Mary again explained the ground rules, and nothing more was said.

Following a time of eating and general activities, Jack interrupted the program and announced in an out-of-breath voice, "We want this evening to be an enjoyable one, but I have found two outside doors to the building propped open with sticks. I don't know who is responsible, but we need to cooperate in observing the rules of the lockin or else we'll all have to go home." The group seemed rather stunned upon hearing this but agreed that they were willing to cooperate in avoiding such an incident happening again. Susan, one of the guest singers, told Mary she had earlier seen several boys coming and going through the door that could not be locked on the inside.

Discussion Disrupted

The next scheduled program item was a discussion on boy-girl relationships entitled "Growing Up Toward Each Other." Tommy, a member of the church but an infrequent attender, was quite outspoken, causing some confusion with his comments and outbursts of laughter during the discussion. He had come to the lockin bringing with him three visitors, Joyce, Mike, and Angela. After the discussion was concluded the "Ghost Run" began. However, Beverly reported to Mary that Tommy and some other boys were causing a disturbance in the back of the auditorium. Mary promptly stopped the them and warned Tommy that if his behavior caused any more difficulties, he would be going home. Tommy replied, "Big deal! Who cares?" and, with a sulking countenance, led the other youth to rejoin the group.

Four Youth Disappear

During free time and refreshments the film "NFL Bloopers" was shown, lasting about thirty minutes. When the lights were turned on, Beverly discovered that Tommy, Joyce, Mike, and Angela were not in the lower auditorium. Tommy's cousin, Doug, was asked if he knew where the four could have gone. Doug said, "No," and that he would go see if Tommy's car was still at the church. The four youth were found inside the car which was parked in the parking lot.

All four youth returned to the lower auditorium and were asked to join Mary and Jack Hunter in a separate room to discuss what was to be done about the situation. Mary gathered some information about each one and discovered that Angela lived nearly twenty miles away in a neighboring community while the other three lived in town. Tommy lived with his father; Joyce was staying the weekend with her grandmother; and Mike lived with his parents.

Three of the youth did not seem concerned about the possibility of being taken or sent home. All Tommy said was, "Call my Dad if you have to, but he won't be happy if you wake him up. If you call him, I'll just get in my car and leave. I don't really care what you do."

Of the four, Angela was the only one pleading, "Please don't call my parents!"

Mary gave Jack Hunter a puzzled look and wondered how she could best handle the situation.

Ponderings for Pedagogy

A familiar activity in youth work is a lockin. Youth and leaders gather one evening and remain throughout the night "locked in" for both security and program reasons. The participants sometimes bring sleeping bags since the program concludes the next morning. Usually the location is a social or recreation area of the church or some other facility rather than a home or elsewhere.

Most leaders in youth ministry contemplate a lockin as a vehicle for such things as building relationships, dealing with issues, having special Bible study, leading spiritual growth experiences, planning youth programs, and just having good fun. Experience teaches that these are not inevitable results, however. Sometimes Murphy's Law seems almost unavoidable in such youth events: "Anything that can go wrong will go wrong." Mary Cauthen may feel a little like that in this case.

There is no authoritative strategy or surefire program for planning an effective lockin. Most often the program is shaped essentially by the personality and creativity of the adult leader(s). Some program planning helps can be found in publications produced by the Sunday School Board of the Southern Baptist Convention.[2]

This case study may be used with professional youth workers as part of a training event to help parents examine the expectations of those leading the youth program, lead lay workers to examine their planning, learn how to attempt conflict resolution, and lead parent-youth-leader trialogue program. Several of these purposes appear in the ideas suggested for guiding the group study of this case.

Group Leadership

Begin by leading the group to identify the persons whose names appear in the case. Calling on specific persons, ask for a brief identification of each one: Who is this person? What do we know about her or him? Record on a chalkboard the names and brief descriptions given. Since the events are not particularly complex, someone may be asked to summarize the lockin story.

Ask, Why is Mary having trouble with this lockin? Lead the group to think about matters such as planning, timing, inviting "outside" youth, adult sponsors, rules, and so forth. Encourage and record the suggestions.

Was the *planning* for this lockin well done? This question opens up discussion of what was actually done and gives people an opportunity to introduce some planning procedures which this youth program may be evaluated. The potential that persons may learn ways to improve planning of other programs, as well as activities in their personal lives, is a long-range value. The following are four techniques for planning.

(1) One technique is called SCAMP and examines objectives:

Specific and concrete,

Consistent with overall purposes or organization,
Attainable,
Measurable, and
Personal to members.[3]

(2) A.M. Adams proposes a decision-making process:
  See—clarify problems.
  Search—look for date possibilities.
  Sort—identify possibilities and prioritize.
  Shape—refine possibilities.
  Settle—make decisive action.[4]

(3) Use NOSE planning:
  Needs (what needs to be done),
  Organization (who does what),
  Strategy (how to), and
  Evaluation (how was it done).

(4) An effective planning process can be built on the following seven steps:

- *Objectives*
    (as many as needed)
    1. never
    2. fully
    3. attainable

- *Goals*
    (as many as needed)
    1. rooted in objectives
    2. measurable
    3. time for completion

- *Action Plans*
    1.   Date ＿＿＿＿＿＿
    2.   Date ＿＿＿＿＿＿
    3.   Date ＿＿＿＿＿＿

- *Organization, council, committee plans*
- *Allocate resources*
- *Evaluate* . . . .
    - process
    - product
    - organization

- *Communicate* . . . rethink

A related issue in planning is the attitude of the pastor of the church. What is the reason for his concern that nothing must cause the church any embarrassment? What is this embarrassment? What is his role in the planning of the event? How would you evaluate the quality and effectiveness of his leadership?

We do most things because they serve some kind of purpose for us. What *purposes* are served by lockins? Why do we have them? After discussion of these general questions, raise the question of the purposes of Mary Cauthen's lockin: What do you think they were? Who set them? Are they clear? Are they explained early enough in the process? Is it failing? Why?

Youth leaders quickly learn that parameters or behavioral limits need to be observed during youth activities and programs. Most often these involve the delicate art of walking a tight rope between too much and too little control or discipline.

What *rules* should govern a lockin? In discussing this question, some thought should be given to *who* should make the rules for a youth activity. Experienced youth leaders find four considerations important: (1) Keep them as simple and few as possible; (2) If at all possible, guide the youth to devise their own, being careful that their rules are appropriate; (3) If formulated and declared, rules must be adhered to by youth and evenhandedly applied by leaders; and (4) Leaders must be careful about making "threats" unless they are prepared to enforce them. Rules must never be used as threats. Everyone should know the penalties for breaking them. Rules should promote order and cooperation, not feelings of oppression.

Issues

Sometimes the issues which underlie a conflict are known but unnamed and unexamined by persons involved in the conflict. What *issues* are involved in this case? Have the discussion group express their ideas in the form of questions. Some issues which may be examined are:

- *Integrity*—Is Mary's *integrity* at stake in the action she takes?
- *Visitors*—How will the handling of the incident affect the image of the way *visitors* are to be treated?
- *Rules*—How strictly are *rules* for behavior to be applied? How will exceptions be made and applied?
- *Parental Consent*—What form of *parental consent* should be obtained for youth events?
- *Balance*—How can one *balance* what is perhaps non-conformist behavior by a few for the good of the larger group and program?
- *Discipline*—To what extent should leadership prepare for and manage *discipline* with youth groups?

The crucial point in this case is the *imminent need for Mary to do something!* She has declared her intent to act. Lead the group to identify her options, from doing nothing, to renegotiating the rules to calling parents. Once options have been recorded, have the group think of the possible consequences of each without judging it "right or wrong." Then ask, What do you now think Mary should do? Keep the focus at this point on how a chosen action will affect Mary's possible future ministry to Tommy, Angela, Mike, and Joyce.

Could this problem have been avoided? If so, how? Responses may include: a different lockin date when more sponsors are available, advance registration, parental permission slips, clear rules announced in advance, no announcement of a quick decision, and a limit set on the number of guests to be admitted.

At some point it may be helpful to consider ways for a leader to act in a conflict situation. In fact, Professor G. Douglass Lewis reports using this case for that very purpose.[5]

Introduce the following five approaches to conflict. Then guide discussion of which is the best choice for Mary and role-play it between Mary and the youth involved.

- "I win. You lose." Competing mode makes winners and losers. It ignores effect on relationships.
- "I give in for the good of our relationship." Accommodation. Preserve relationship at expense of one's personal goals.
- "I want out. I give up." Avoiding. Cannot achieve goals so get away from conflict.
- "I will meet you half way." Lose/lose. Get and give something. Preserve relationship.
- "I win. You Win." is collaboration. Goals of both sides taken seriously. Mutual problem-solving. Goals and relationships maintained. Choice is negotiation. All factors become "ours."[6]

Searching for Grace

Human relationships have resources or aids which can assist in dealing with daily living as well as crises. Christians will see these as God-given resources of grace. They are gifts (*charis*—things freely given) whose discovery should facilitate their use in personal living and problem-solving. "This refers to God's grace that supplies the gift of persons, concepts, and sources of faith that may assist one in making responsible and loving decisions."[7] Consider the following:

- Does God's forgiveness of us create the need to forgive others? Can forgiveness be given without threatening our egos or personhood? How? Can this be applied to the situation in this case?
- How may parents become members of the healing team which exists within the church as the family of God? How can they be enabled to do so?
- What concepts, teachings, and clues may be discovered in the Bible for effective conflict resolution?
- Seeing prayer as addressing both God and fellow persons, is there a role in this case for prayer which is free both of attempts at manipulation and gaining advantage?
- Examine implications for possible actions by Mary in terms of

their potential effect on the church's outreach and mission to youth and adults. Does this consideration always, sometimes, almost never, or rarely rank as a priority consideration? Why? Should it?

Parental Permission Slips

Most youth leaders recognize the importance of securing parental permission for youth to attend events such as lockins, retreats, camps, trips, and so forth. Two samples are follow. The "General Release" form was developed and used by Second Avenue Baptist Church of Rome, Georgia. The second form was developed by Frankie Wiley.

General Release

STATE OF
COUNTY OF
KNOW ALL MEN BY THESE Presents, that I/we
_____ in consideration of the sum of One Dollar ($1.00) and other good and valuable consideration, the receipt of which is hereby acknowledged, do hereby remise, release and forever discharge _____ Church of _____, its agents and successors, of and from all and all manner of actions, causes of actions, suits, proceedings, debts, dues, contracts, judgments, damages, claims and demands whatsoever in law or equity, which against the said _____ Church I ever had, now have or which I, my heirs, executors, or administrators hereafter can, shall, or my have for or by reason of any matter, cause or thing whatsoever, including but not limited to, responsibility for my child in the event of any accident, injury or death during the (year and event) of the said _____ Church, from now and in the future.

IN WITNESS WHEREOF, I have hereunto set my hand and seal the _____ day of _____, (year).
_____   _____ (Seal)
Witness

_____
_____ (Seal) Witness

Release of Physical Responsibility

I hereby release _____ Church and all adult chaperons from responsibility for my child in event of any

accident,   injury,   or   death   during   the   church   sponsored
_____. (event and date)

I also give my permission to administer to my child any needed medical attention due to injury or sickness.

Please list all medical allergies:

Please list any special health problems:

Date of last tetanus injection:

Signed:

_____

Parents or legal guardians

Please fill out the above information about your son/daughter. Should an emergency occur this permission will facilitate prompt attention to any needs which arise. Return the completed form as soon as possible.

12

Lisa's Disappearance[1]

Anxiety was apparent in the words of Frank Bell. "Ron, I think I need to call Pastor Wyatt and alert him to the situation so that he can contact Lisa's parents. They need to know that she has not been seen in seven hours."

"Yes, I guess Dr. Wyatt does need to be told. Also, tell him that we called the hospitals, and the police have issued an all points bulletin. The county sheriff is on notice, and the dean of student affairs and dean of admissions have been contacted. Assure him that we will immediately relay any new information as it becomes available," Ron replied. "I'll stay here with the group and try to keep calm so the kids can enjoy the concert."

Trip to Mercer

Ron Kirkland was serving as minister of youth at Belleview Baptist Church, Murfreesboro, Tennessee. He had completed his undergraduate work at Mercer University, a Baptist school in Macon, Georgia.

The New Eden Singers from Mercer University had recently presented a concert at Belleview while on tour. A popular Christian singing group, the New Eden Singers made a striking impression on many of the youth at Belleview. As a result, several of the older youth had expressed an interest in attending Mercer after they finished high school. At least two members of Belleview were also graduates of Mercer, and their added interest encouraged Ron to plan a visit to the Mercer campus so the interested youth could see the school first hand.

When final plans for the trip were completed, the group consisted of twenty high school sophomores, juniors, and seniors (Ron had decided to include any interested high schoolers, even sophomores). Accompanying the group as chaperones were Frank and Mary Ann Bell, George and Carolyn Landers, and Ken Young, the church bus driver. Frank and Mary Ann Bell were especially interested in the trip because their son, Jeff, had already been accepted for enrollment in the next fall term, and the three of them could visit together.

The bus left Murfreesboro at about noon on Thursday and arrived in Macon at 9:00 p.m., a little later than expected because of rainy weather. As the group checked into the motel, George and Carolyn Landers announced to Ron that they would be staying with George's brother in Macon. Ron nodded, saying, "OK . . . I guess it will be all right," and trying rather unsuccessfully to hide his disapproval.

After breakfast on Friday morning, Ron assembled the group at 9:00 a.m. for a brief orientation. He reminded them that everyone would have lunch together in the cafeteria at noon and "specifically instructed" everyone to be on the bus at 1:00 p.m. to return to the motel. The youth were given the responsibility of deciding for themselves which classes, buildings, or activities they would like to visit. Three youth decided to visit a class that was meeting that morning. The others left in small groups to see the campus, play table games at the student center, or "just to goof around."

The Late Lisa

After lunch the group began gathering at the bus, and by 1:00 p.m. everyone was present, with one exception—Lisa Collins. A high school senior and president of the youth council, Lisa was friendly, energetic, and very popular among the youth. Ron had thought at times that she was a little "boy crazy" but valued her leadership in the council. He had spoken with her just a few minutes before everyone began to board the bus and had mentioned that the bus would be leaving shortly. At that time Lisa was talking with a young man named Chris Harned, a student at Mercer and a member of the New Eden Singers. Chris and Lisa met when the singers visited Belleview.

Ron kept the bus waiting until 1:30 p.m., then decided that rather than inconvenience the whole group any further they would travel back to the motel and wait for a call from Lisa. He wondered if she had decided to visit some afternoon classes. Though irritated, he refused to be unduly alarmed when she did not rejoin the group or contact him early in the afternoon.

Dinner and Concert

Following some group discussions and recreation in the afternoon, the group was scheduled to have dinner at 6:00 p.m., then proceed to the university auditorium to attend a campus-wide concert by the New Eden Singers at 7:00 p.m. Ron had decided to hold the tickets for the entire group until they entered the auditorium; therefore, it was necessary for the whole group to be together in order to gain admittance. The concert was part of a larger emphasis weekend planned by the college.

By dinner time, Ron still did not consider the events of the afternoon to be a crisis because he trusted Lisa. However, he was now worried and puzzled that Lisa would fail to inform him or any of the chaperones or her friends of her plans. Ron had told the chaperones of his concern and emphasized the need to be even more alert to any indication as to her whereabouts. He was now beginning to feel the weight of responsibility for Lisa's safety to a much greater degree.

Following dinner, the group boarded the bus for the ride to the concert hall. After getting the group seated and then conferring with Frank Bell, Ron decided to slip out and telephone the dean of student affairs (who had helped arrange the trip) and the dean of admissions (a personal friend) and inform them of his concern for Lisa. He told them she was last seen with Chris Harned at 1:00 p.m.

On returning to the concert, Ron was told by Frank Bell: "I am getting worried that something terrible could have happened to Lisa." Ron knew that his own concern had probably spilled over into the entire group. He could sense increasing anxiety about Lisa among some of the older youth, as well as among the chaperones.

Legal Authorities Notified

Meanwhile, the dean of student affairs had notified the county sheriff and the Macon Police Department, which had issued an all points bulletin on Lisa and Chris. All local hospital admissions were also checked, with negative results.

Ron and Frank then decided that Lisa's parents, Jim and Sue Collins, must be informed about the situation. During the concert Frank made several unsuccessful attempts to reach Dr. John Wyatt by phone. Wyatt was the pastor of Belleview and knew Jim and Sue Collins well, since they were active members of the church. When he finally reached the Wyatt home, Frank discovered Dr. Wyatt was not there. He explained the situation to Joyce Wyatt and requested that she ask Dr. Wyatt to consider calling Lisa's parents when he came in and that he remain available for further telephone consultation. Frank asked that she not call Lisa's parents, thinking that Lisa might reappear before the pastor came home.

Ron remained with the youth while Frank placed the calls. During intermission, he tried to appear relaxed and to reassure the youth group that everything would be all right. It was obvious that one or two older youth were not satisfied by his words, though.

Lisa Reappears

The concert was over at 11:30, and there was still no sign of Lisa and Chris, who had not shown up to sing at the concert. Ron instruct-

ed Frank and the other chaperones to return to the bus and wait while
he make one or two phone calls. After learning there was no new word
from the dean or the police, Ron walked back toward the bus feeling
frightened and upset; the situation was now critical, he thought.

Upon arriving at the bus, Ron found Lisa standing by the door, crying and surrounded by the youth and chaperones. She kept insisting,
"We haven't done anything." Ron assured her that, at the moment,
the most important thing was her safety and that she was back with
the group. Ron and Frank agreed that any further discussion of the
incident should be delayed until after they got home. Everyone was so
relieved and happy that Lisa was safe that they seemed to want to
forgive and forget.

Ron hurriedly called Dr. Wyatt to inform him of Lisa's safe return. Dr.
Wyatt had arrived home only moments before Ron's call, which
meant, fortunately, that he had not had time to call Lisa's parents. Dr.
Wyatt and Ron thought it best not to notify her parents of the day's
events by phone.

However, Ron advised Lisa that a conference with him and Dr. Wyatt would be necessary in view of her display of irresponsibility. Lisa
agreed while sniffling into her handkerchief.

The next morning the group returned to Murfreesboro.

Jim and Sue Collins

Lisa told her parents about some of the events that had taken place,
but as Ron later learned, she intentionally failed to tell them that Ron
had been forced to alert campus and law enforcement officials or of
the distress she had cause the others. Lisa preferred that her parents,
particularly her mother, only have limited knowledge of the problems
she had created on the trip. In fact, Ron had previously noticed what
he interpreted as an absence of warmth between Lisa and Sue
Collins.

Lisa's parents had always been rather strict with her, especially
when it came to dating. Her mother had even asked her, in the presence of one young man, not to hold hands in their living room. Lisa's
father always seemed to play a secondary, almost passive role in their
home life, Ron felt. Jim's health was not good, and he had been out of
work for an extended period of time. An ordained minister, he had previously been employed in a staff position at a denominational residential facility for needed, orphaned children and youth.

Sunday Morning

The next day (Sunday), Lisa stopped Ron in the hall at church.
"Ron, I want to ask a real favor. *Please* don't tell my parents any more

about the trip than you have to. Just tell them enough to satisfy them. *Please!*"

Ron replied: "Before agreeing to anything like that, I think you, the pastor, and I need to do a lot of talking. So I have scheduled a conference for the three of us at 4:00 p.m. Wednesday. Is that acceptable?" Lisa nodded in agreement.

The Conference

During the next three days, Ron was somewhat surprised that Lisa's parents made no attempt to discuss the incident with him. Nevertheless, he wanted to talk with Lisa before approaching her parents. Thus, on Wednesday afternoon, Lisa, Dr. Wyatt, and Ron gathered to discuss the events during the trip to Mercer.

How could Lisa be helped to make an objective evaluation of her actions in light of her relationship with parents, friends, and herself? What should her parents be told? Were her actions a type of running away behavior? What kind of help did Lisa need? Should she be expected to do or say anything as "reparation"? These were among the questions Ron and Dr. Wyatt had discussed in preparation for the conference. Yet as Ron invited Lisa into his office on Wednesday afternoon, he felt uncertain as to how he should guide the conversation.

Ponderings for Pedagogy

Though written for stepparents, Evelyn Felker's book, *Raising Other People's Kids*, suggests one aspect of the role of anyone who works with young people.[2] There are times when you find yourself being forced to deal with traditional *parental* tasks—like getting everyone in the car on time, knowing where everyone is at the moment, overseeing "feeding times," and worrying when they don't come back at a given time. The phrase *in loco parentis* means to be and act in the place of or in the role of a parent. Every youth worker knows how it feels, including Ron Kirkland.

The other perspective on these responsibilities is the viewpoint of the youth involved, often expressed as "Why can't you see that being with a boy friend or girl friend is sometimes more important than anything else? What are you worrying about? You know I can take care of myself. You just don't trust me!" Indeed, in their legitimate anxiety about the safety and well-being of their children, parents often find it difficult to know when and how to loosen their grip on a growing adolescent.

This case presents both of these perspectives within the context of a college campus visit by a group of church youth and their chaperones. It adds the interests and involvement of youth peers, adults, and parents to the equation of a singular youth-adult interaction—that of Ron and Lisa.

Obvious uses for this case study include those settings and types already suggested for several of the other cases in this text. Further, it is very effective as a vehicle for leading *youth* to think about responsibility, discipline, group covenants, peers, and their leaders. *Leaders* find the case helpful in examining their roles, responsibilities, and learning about intervention and counseling possibilities. *Parents* discover in the case aspects of their accountability in youth programs and through dialogue can become more aware of and sympathetic to some of the stresses and problems of youth leaders.

A positive, rather than negative, value of this case is its use as a proactive effort to avoid problems like those in this church youth group. This can be accomplished by using the case as a means of discussing, formulating, and clarifying guidelines for conduct *before* a trip or other overnight experience. In light of the chaperones who did not stay overnight with the group, it seems also appropriate that "expected behavior" would apply to chaperones as well.

Group Leadership

To introduce this case, ask the discussion group to name and give facts which are known about each person in the case. Probe the perceptions of the group about each of these person. Now choose one of the following two ideas as a way to continue the discussion.

Ask for a volunteer or call on a specific person to answer: "If you had been Ron Kirkland when Lisa and Chris reappeared at the bus, what would you have said? Done?" After the response ask, "Do others of you agree with that? What would you have done or said differently? . . . Why do you feel that way?" Another approach is to ask three people to role play the conversation between Ron, Lisa, and Chris at the time of the reappearance. Let the role play continue ten to fifteen minutes before intervening. Then encourage consideration of how each player expressed the views of his or her character.

Guide the group to think about the various developments in the case. "Why did things happen as they did? What would explain the factors that either permitted or even encouraged events to turn out this way?" It will be helpful to ensure that the ideas suggested include (1) the freedom Ron permitted the youth, (2) the trust level granted to the group, (3) the strict attitude of Lisa's parents, and (4) the degree of self-determination allowed the youth group (specific data?). In the discussion, avoid letting simplistic or single factors be blamed for Lisa's behavior.

Issues

Seen in its totality, "Lisa's Disappearance" contains several issues. The evidence for good *planning* of the event can be examined. Another issues is the question of the *value* of youth trips. Are they worth the effort and expense? What purposes do they serve? Attention can also focus on the *responsibility* of youth with relation to other persons and plans involved in a group experience. The role and importance of *chaperones*—type of person, ratio to number of youth, duties, and so forth— can also be examined. Lisa's *family system* and her parents' attitudes are factors which underlie her development and relationships to authority figures.

Situations such as those in this case suggest an important principle which needs to be considered for working with youth. Youth groups sometimes have one or more members who seem to feel that their desires and preferences *should have priority* over those of leaders and other group members. The question raised by their actions is: To what degree should a person or small minority within a youth group be allowed to act in ways which supersede or dominate the good of the larger number involved? Lisa and Chris's actions raise this issue—she for the youth of Belleview and he for the New Eden Singers.

Ask: "What *issues* are fundamental to the events?" Among those which may be proposed are personal responsibility, family relationships, what transpired between Chris and Lisa, Pastor Wyatt's role, the long-range effect on other youth, role of chaperones, and Ron's responsibility to Lisa's parents. Each issue suggested by the group should be recorded and discussed as necessary and desirable.

Since a conference has already been scheduled between the pastor, Lisa, and Ron, ask the group: "Let's build a list of things which Ron and Dr. Wyatt should decide to talk about with Lisa. What would you want on the agenda?" It is appropriate at this point to ask: "Why do you suppose they waited so long before talking with Lisa? Was that wise? Why?" Then work on the items to be discussed with Lisa and the likely effect each one will have on her and the other youth.

Dale Francis, a widely experienced counselor to families with grown children, advises parents to follow guidelines in dealing with their youth. Francis's ideas can be helpful for the conversations with Lisa by church staff and with other parents of youth.

- Don't feel guilty.
- Don't argue (but make clear your firm convictions).
- Don't say they "owe it to me."
- Don't disown them.
- Do stay close to them.

- Do stay close to God.
- Do leave a door open.[3]

Conclude the discussion by leading participants to suggest some implications of Lisa's case for the youth of their group. Ideas could include responsibility to one another, problems experienced by parents, role of church staff members, and forgiveness.

Resources of Grace

The church context for this entire case makes potential sources of grace more obvious. Priestly and pastoral roles of Ron and Dr. Wyatt, relationships, belonging, a caring congregation, youth group, the church context ant its symbols (the conference between Ron, Dr. Wyatt, and Lisa takes place at church), prayer, and Lisa's apparent contrition serve as channels for God's grace. The ministry of grace needs to extend beyond the events of the campus visit into Lisa's home experience and the relationships between her and her parents.

Part 3
Choosing and Using Case Studies

While there are spontaneous and unstructured ways to introduce and use case studies, considerable experience suggests the wisdom of a more careful and studied approach if their fullest values are to be realized. Let's look, therefore, at some types of cases, selection, case teaching, and evaluation of case teaching.

Types of Cases

There are two basic types of cases: contrived and genuine (real). Of course these contain numerous subvarieties which nevertheless remain within these two basic types.

An extensive listing of types of case studies was developed by Le-Roy Ford in *Using Case Studies in Teaching and Training*. His twelve categories include: classical case, unfinished story, embryo case, critical incident, cartoon teaser case, "mail basket" case, "baited" case, "impromptu" case, *ex post facto* case, educational simulation, informational "what-do-you-see" case, and psychological "what-do-you-see" case.[1] Ford's explanation of each type is skillfully developed and artfully explained through cartoons and a filmstrip which accompanies his text. Also included are fifteen values or purposes for using case studies.

Other types which can be added to his categories are: autobiographical and biographical, diaries, interview verbatims (like "Ron Scanlon, Teenager"), illustrations, incidents reported in a newspaper or other printed sources, and audiovisuals.

The case study as a research tool is best seen through its use in recent years in morals and values education. Harvard's Lawrence Kohlberg developed his well-known "Heinz Dilemma" case which asks whether a man who is without money and needs medicine for his dying wife is justified in burglarizing the drugstore after the druggist refuses help. The text of the story is as follows:

> In Europe a woman was near death from cancer. One drug might save her, a form of radium that a druggist in the same town had recently discovered. The druggist was charging $2,000 (ten times what the drug

cost him to make). The sick woman's husband, Heinz, went to everyone he knew to borrow the money, but he could get together only about half of what it cost. He told the druggist that his wife was dying and asked him to sell it cheaper or let him pay later. But the druggist said no. The husband got desperate and broke into the man's store to steal the drug for his wife. Should the husband have done that? Why?[2]

This and other cases reflecting a similar model are used extensively in efforts to identify stages in the development of morals and "values clarification" in children and youth. Kohlberg has also worked out a scheme of "stages" and "levels" for such thinking in children and youth.

Educators Leland Howe, Howard Kirschenbaum, Sidney Simon, and others have likewise developed and used cases with such titles as "The Alligator Story," "The Fall-Out Shelter Problem," "The Pie of Life," and so forth to enable children and youth to examine their values and perhaps to aid in developing more positive ones.[3] Other educators such as Ted Ward and James Fowler have used similar techniques to study faith development.

The cases in this book reflect a structure and methodology adapted from those developed and used by the Harvard Graduate School of Business and the Case Method Institute, which was latter developed through the Association of Theological Schools. The fundamental characteristic of this approach is that the case must present a problem situation confronted and lived through by *real persons*, not fictional ones. These persons essentially said, did, and experienced what is reported by them or understood by the case writer to have actually occurred. Each case represents the effort of an experiencing person to describe reality as he or she knows it.

Selection

Selection of particular cases for use in youth ministry involves many factors. The following are some important ones to consider.

● The learning goal of the leader and group helps to focus the search. Will it cause participants to consider issues (moral, ethical, theological, and so forth)? Does it lend itself to differences of opinion about these issues and the actions to be taken by persons in the case?

● If one wants them, are research materials readily available to enrich understanding and aid discussion? Are new ideas and possibilities likely to be generated by the case? Is it suitable for the sophistication and maturity level of the learners?

● If there is more than a single case available for use, examine the level of conflict and progression of the cases and choose the one which best meets your purposes and presenting skills.

- Carefully consider the complexity of the case. It should not be so great as to impede the understanding necessary to good group discussion and wide participation. Often a brief (one- or two-page) case can prove as provocative and helpful a learning tool as longer, more complex ones.

- Best results usually are achieved when the teacher feels comfortable discussing and presenting the case. This comfort level may occur only after teaching the case several times, or it can develop on the first use of the case.

- Be prepared to experiment with new cases when they are discovered and available. Some leaders tend to reuse and even overuse the cases they like best. This practice meets the leader's needs while those of group members may be neglected.

- Avoid using a case where persons in the case could be recognized by someone in the group, even though protection of privacy and maintenance of anonymity are always goals of a case writer. If such use is contemplated, check with the person(s) first and see if permission can be secured. Always protect the true identity of persons described in the case, even though case writers *always* use false names for persons, cities, churches, locations, and so forth.

However, veteran case writers Robert and Alice Evans tell of teaching a case involving a widow whose husband had committed suicide only to discover when she introduced herself that the real "Mary Matthews" of their case was present. With a tear-streaked face, she told them: "I must confess this discussion is the most helpful thing that has happened to me since he died!" The Evanses concluded we should not "underestimate the healing and reconciling power of honest dialogue in which the Spirit's presence could allow Mary to find a new kind of wisdom about herself, and trust for other members of the Christian family."[4] The central person in one of my own cases asked to be present and even identified when I taught "his" case.

- Always be on the lookout for resources and techniques which can enrich your teaching and leadership of case studies. Consider possibilities in role play, voting, film, filmstrips, statistics, simulated telephone conversations, debates, panels, and so forth.

- Be alert to case possibilities which you can research and write to meet needs of your youth group, leaders, a conference, a workshop, or parents of youth. Generate your own case material through sensitive observation, adequate research, and good writing. Remember always maintain anonymity for persons, places, organizations, and so forth by using pseudonyms and changing identifying data.

Case Teaching

What kind of preparation for teaching a case should be made by a good case teacher? To answer this is to run the risk of appearing to know the "one way to do case studies" when it does not exist. However, there are several suggestions which are rooted in considerable experience.

Know the *facts* specifically, thoroughly, and in every possible detail. You should not need to look at the case during discussion of it. If facts are being incorrectly stated or assumed by a group member, you may want to reply, "Is that what she really said? Do others of you agree?"

Prepare a general framework or teaching outline for the discussion but be prepared also to alter it as the group process dictates. Put this plan into outline form and write it on paper, building it around such considerations as:

● How should I begin? What should I say first? How can I create interest?

● What is will be my overall development of the case discussion? How shall I identify some major considerations which should not be overlooked?

● What are all the *issues* I can identify in the case? Can these be put into groups (relationships, legal, family, theological)?

Two matters need careful attention here. One, be certain to probe deeply enough to separate underlying issues from immediate or precipitating factors. These are not the same. For example, in "The Bake Sale" case the precipitating incident is the vetoing by Tyson Duncan of the effort by youth to raise funds through a bake sale and the resulting conflict which could destroy youth ministry in the church. The issues are matters like the role of youth in the church, generation relationships, youth-adult relationships, the nature and mission of a church, power, and so forth.

Two, guard against manipulating others into merely accepting your identification of issues. Help group members struggle with their own listing of issues. The leader's list should simply help participants probe additional possibilities.

● Identify possible actions or "solutions" in the case. Include every possibility which can be imagined regardless of how unlikely it may seem at first appear. Then for each possibility try to identify the *what if* implications of each action, the advantages, disadvantages, risks, and so forth. Be prepared to recognize that there are other actions which group members may suggest which have not occurred to you. Always avoid pressing *your* ideas.

During the discussion, respond to all comments and suggestions which are proposed, without evaluation. Writing these on a chalkboard, newsprint, or overhead cel helps to identify the contributor and preserve the contribution for further injection into the discussion. Further, it makes connections among ideas possible, as well as demonstrating similarities and dissimilarities between them. Lastly, the leader can return to them by saying, "Is that also what Larry was saying over here? Would you agree, Larry?" or "Why? Help us by elaborating on that."

Concentrate on calling persons by first names when possible. Some leaders do this easily, having a good facility for remembering names. Leaders who are not so gifted sometimes distribute name tags for use until they are better acquainted with group members. Knowing first names enables the leader to bring people into the discussion by such comments as: "Bob, would you agree to that? Phyllis, is that opposite to what you expressed a few moments ago? Jim, how do you feel about Ann's suggestion?"

Respect, accept, and affirm all points of view. Do not "take sides" with any person or viewpoint expressed. Let persons be free to say what they truly feel, think, and believe without risking your disapproval or disagreement. Encourage expressions of insights that are different. If this creates differences of opinion or even conflict, heighten and use it to facilitate learning.

Move discussion along but do not rush the process. Rushing the discussion creates suspicion that the discussants are simply engaged in a game designed and controlled by the leader rather than being involved in their own creative learning enterprise. Good insights usually require some incubation time and/or "trial runs" at verbalization.

During the study and discussion process, information given in the written case should be the sole data for analysis and learning. In cases written by (or when additional facts are known by) the leader, there is always a temptation to introduce such information and allow it to impact the leader's guidance of the discussion. Resist that temptation! As with the discussants, deal only with what is in the case. A related effect of introducing new information is that discussants then want to know, "How did it turn out? What happened to her?" Such inquiries should be answered, if at all, only after the case discussion has been completed.

Cases are a little like a good mystery story in that they present facts as seen and experienced by the primary character. These facts are usually "subjective" to that person. Therefore, a case can present information to the reader in a way which may appear odd, strange, or even questionable. You may be thinking *no one would say that*" or *I cannot believe this*. Determine to practice the art of enjoying a good mystery. Called "the willing suspension of disbelief," it is a way of accepting and dealing with the facts as presented rather than how we think they should or might be.

Ensure that physical provisions in the room facilitate the group process. Arrange chairs and equipment so that they enable participants to be on the front row rather than behind others (where they may feel hidden and uninvolved). The circle or U-shape is a good design.

Note also that it is wise at times to move people into different patterns. For instance, you may suggest, "Boys stand up and move at least ten feet to the right and be seated. Girls, stand and move five feet to your right and be seated." Or "All persons on this half of the room move directly across to the person opposite you and find a way to be seated next to him or her." Or, "Everyone walk around the room looking up. When you look down, go and sit by the first person with whom you make eye contact." Of course, it is also helpful at times to arrange chairs in small groups for particular kinds of desirable discussion and response. While simple to do, such methods can increase involvement, help avoid some energy lows during discussion, and help to rearrange social cliques and subgroups.

Like other case teachers, I have found that moving around in the room during the discussion is helpful. Standing near, alongside, or even behind a contributor in the group can encourage and strengthen his/her participation and views, especially if it is a minority opinion. You may want to even "help" this participant by arguing his or her case against a majority or opposing view. Sometimes it is convenient and helpful to be seated by the person for a period of time. Such techniques help to underscore that the dialogue is *between the discussants* rather than with you as the leader.

Positioning oneself in a section of the group which has been quiet or unresponsive can encourage participation. It also is helpful to ask, "Bill, what do you think about that? Or, Sara, how do you feel about that suggestion?" This lets persons know their input is both desired and important.

Case studies can create frustration among discussants because the proposed "answers" do not "solve" the problems to everyone's satisfaction. Here is yet another way in which cases genuinely mirror life which teaches us that progress consists in correcting old mistakes by risking the making of new ones. In reality life is a succession of ambiguities and interrelated problems-in-resolution rather than a string of simple and complete answers for every difficulty.

As we face life's problems and decisions—our own and those of others—something within makes us hope that a way to cope can be found. We feel, "Surely there must be some way to handle this."

When the problem belongs to someone else we may wish we could help them find a solution, a "happy ending." However, good cases are more aligned with the reality that we usually must make decisions which are not always perfect solutions, either for now or for all time. However, many of the issues and rationale for actions can be timeless. This is so with good cases.

Case discussions sometimes degenerate into multiple speeches by a small handful of talkative (or overly talkative) persons. Here are some workable ways to cope with this problem: (1) "Good. Does anyone else have a suggestion?" (2) "Now let's hear from someone who hasn't spoken. Jim, what about you? How do you feel about it?" (3) "Let's agree that no person can speak more than once until *everyone* has had a chance to speak." (4) "For the first seven minutes only males in our group can speak. Then females may speak for seven minutes. After that, anyone may speak. Mabel, would you time us?" (5) Choose six persons, equally divided between male and female and including some persons not likely to speak otherwise, and write their names on the chalkboard. Say: "To begin our discussion, I am asking that no one else speak until we have heard from these persons. The rest of you are asked to listen and think until your turn comes."

The final goal is for people to be set free to think for themselves and find their own rather than someone else's solutions for life's problems. The apostle Paul taught self-responsibility rather than "salvation by works" when he proposed that each of us must "work out your own salvation with fear and trembling" (Phil. 2:12, RSV). The emphasis is on one's own personal search for the meaning of salvation for day-to-day living and decision making. That is both good theology and good Christian education, and the cases are an excellent resource for doing both.

Have a prayer and ask that the Holy Spirit empower and use the case, making it come alive as a vehicle to aid youth, parents, and leaders to cope more successfully with concerns in their own lives. Yearn and work that they may ardently search for the truth that "will make you free" (John 8:32, RSV).

Evaluating Case Teaching

Like beauty, whether a case study is good or not is in the eye of the beholder (the reader, the leader, discussants). All of these persons can help evaluate a case and the teaching processes used with a group of learners. Several ideas for receiving feedback which can aid in evaluating case studies follow.

Reader

As persons read, discuss, and reflect on cases, lead them to ask questions about the case itself.

1. Is the case clearly written? Well reported?
2. Can I easily follow the "time line" of development for the events?
3. Are characters in the case adequately presented?
4. Are actions and possible issues helpfully described?
5. What action options seem available?
6. Do I feel some rising interest in the events of the case? Would I like to share, discuss, or even argue, these events with others?

Leader

Helpful ways to examine how one's teaching of a case has gone is to tape or record the session for later study, use a person to serve as a recorder/listener, and have a general discussion with group members in a debriefing session. Such techniques can produce new ideas for improving teaching-learning processes.

Discussants

Two examples are offered for how feedback may be obtained from discussants. One is to reserve sufficient time after the discussion to request immediate verbal responses. While each leader will want to shape the questions to be used, here are some ideas.

● Were there facts or information you needed and did not have? Was the case unclear about anything?

● How did the leader handle the structure of the discussion? Too much structure? Not enough?

● Did the leader give adequate attention to all suggestions and comments? Equal time? Was partiality shown to any one person, idea, or position?

● Was response in the group balanced? Did anyone dominate the discussion? Speak only once? Was there anyone who did not speak? Did subgroups appear within the larger group? (By tape recording the session and listening to it later, such facts can be revealed.)

● What body language from the leader do you recall? At what points? Did it affect you and how?

● Were you pleased with the use made of the chalkboard, newsprint, overhead projector, and so forth? Suggestions for improvement?

● What have you/we learned from this case? Useful process? In what way?

A second idea involves a somewhat more formal process for evaluating study of a case by a group. Participants are asked to assist the discussion leader by completing a printed questionnaire. Make it clear that their purpose is to help improve the learning process rather than to criticize the leader or group members. Respondents may remain anonymous. Some leaders feel this is best because, they believe, it encourages group members to be more honest and helpful than if their identities were known.

On the other hand, if the leader knows the person completing the evaluation form, it can help him to judge the seriousness and validity of the observations. Further, should the leader want more feedback or discussion about specific comments, it is easily secured from the contributors.

Another way to use this technique is to ask an outside observer to assist as evaluator-consultant. Before tje session discuss the case to be taught and your objectives for its use. Have this observer sit as unobtrusively as possible in the room and fill out the questionnaire as the discussion proceeds. The observer should refrain from participating in the case discussion, making possible the fullest concentration on the process. Soon after the teaching session, the leader should meet with the evaluator for feedback and discussion.

Two written instruments have also been developed for use in evaluation. One was developed by Garth Rossell of Gordon Conwell Theological Seminary. One of its strengths is that it enables a single observer to track the varying energy and participation levels observable throughout the teaching-discussion process.

The second instrument (see below) was developed by the author, has been used with a number of discussion groups, and can be used by all participants in the case study and/or an external evaluator-consultant.

Feedback on Case Study Teaching
Case Title _____

1. Teacher preparation appeared to be: 1=excellent, 2=good, 3=acceptable, 4=fair, 5=adequate, 6=poor
   (circle one)   1   2   3   4   5   6
   Remarks: _____
2. The way (technique, process, and so forth) the session was introduced or begun
                     1   2   3   4   5   6
   Remarks _____
3. The phrasing, forming, and use of questions by teacher was
                     1   2   3   4   5   6
   Remarks: _____
4. In-depth probing of participants' insights into the case material was

         1   2   3   4   5   6

Remarks: _____

5. Comments/contribution of participants were interrelated, sometimes even pointed out contradictory view(s) of others, and were used to aid discussion.

         1   2   3   4   5   6

Remarks: _____

6. The discussion appeared to have structure and move toward some final resolution, without inhibiting discussion.

         1   2   3   4   5   6

Remarks: _____

7. Techniques were used (role play, conversations simulated, counseling acted out, voting, call for evidence) to aid the discussion.

         1   2   3   4   5   6

Remarks: _____

8. Teacher appeared sensitive and alert to the implication of comments (in the case and by participants) and "teased" them out in the discussion process.

         1   2   3   4   5   6

Remarks: _____

9. Possible "solutions" or actions by persons in the case and their implications were considered.

         1   2   3   4   5   6

Remarks: _____

10. What I liked most and found most helpful in this case:

_____

_____

11. I would rate the case and the teaching as:

     Case   1   2   3   4   5   6   Comment:

     Teaching   1   2   3   4   5   6   Comment:

12. Additional suggestions from you are encouraged and welcome.

         Evaluator _____

                    (Signed)

Notes

Part 1

1. Adapted from listings given by Junior League Review and from a CBS News program, both in 1987.

2. Anthony Campolo, *Growing Up in America* (Grand Rapids: Zondervan, 1989), 69.

3. Source unknown.

4. Eda J. LeShan, *How to Survive Parenthood* (New York: Random House, 1965), 3-20.

5. *New Standard Bible Dictionary,* 3d rev. ed. (New York: Funk and Wagnalls Co., 1936), 680.

6. Lewis J. Sherrill, *The Rise of Christian Education* (New York: Macmillan Co., 1944), 50.

7. James William McClendon, Jr., *Biography as Theology: How Life Stories Can Remake Theology* (Nashville: Abingdon Press, 1974), 13.

8. John S. Dunn, *A Search for God in Time and Memory* (London: Macmillan Co., 1969), ix, 169, 179.

9. R. Alan Culpepper, "Story and History in the Gospels," *Review and Expositor* 131 (Summer 1984): 469*f*.

10. Ibid, 472.

11. Ross Snyder, *Young People and Their Culture* (Nashville: Abingdon Press, 1969), 109*f*.

12. Malcolm P. McNair, ed., *The Case Method at the Harvard Business School* (New York: McGraw-Hill Book Co., 1954), preface.

13. Paul Cozby, *Methods in Behavioral Research*, 3d ed. (Palo Alto, Calif.: Mayfield Publishing Co., 1985), 127.

14. John W. M. Rothney, *The High School Student: A Book of Cases* (New York: Holt, Rinehart and Winston, 1953).

15. *Woe is Me!: Case Studies in Moral Dilemmas* (Nashville: The Sunday School Board of the Southern Baptist Convention, 1969), 4.

16. Statement from Krister Stendahl's lecture at Case Method Institute, Episcopal Theological Seminary, Boston, July 1974.

Case 1

1. Joseph Adelson, "Adolescence and the Generalization Gap," *Psychology Today*, February 1979, 33.

2. Joseph Adelson, ed., *Handbook of Adolescent Psychology* (New York: Wiley, 1980), 3-46.

3. Adelson, "Adolescence and the Generalization Gap," 37.

4. Amitai Etzioni, "Youth Is Not a Class," *Psychology Today*, February 1978, 20.

5. David Elkind, *All Grown Up and No Place to Go* (Reading, Mass.: Addison-Wesley, 1984), 5.

6. Ibid., 1.

7. Gerald R. Adams and Thomas Gullotta, *Adolescent Life Experiences* (Monterey, Calif.: Brooks/Cole Publishing Co., 1983), 252f.

8. "American Divorce Rate Exaggerated, Pollster Says," *The Courier-Journal*, June 29, 1987, section A, 4.

9. J. S. Wallerstein and J. B. Kelly wrote four research studies: "The Effects of Parental Divorce: The Adolescent Experience," *The Child in His Family: Children at Psychiatric Risk*, ed. Anthony James Elwyn and Cyrille Koupernik, (New York: Wiley, 1974); "The Effects of Parental Divorce: Experiences of the Child in Late Latency," *American Journal of Orthopsychiatry* 46 (April 1976): 256-69; "Effects of Divorce on the Visiting Father-Child Relationship," *American Journal of Psychiatry* 137 (December 1980), 1534-39; "Surviving the Breakup: How Children and Parents Cope with Divorce" (New York: Basic, 1980).

10. R. A. Kulka and H. Weingarten, "The Long Term Effects of Parental Divorce in Childhood on Adult Adjustment," *Journal of Social Issues* 33 (Fall 1979): 50-78.

11. T. Parish and J. Taylor, "The Impact of Divorce and Subsequent Father Absence on Children's and Adolescents' Self-Concepts," *Journal of Youth and Adolescence* 8 (December 1979): 427-32. E. Young and T. Parish, "Impact of Father Absence During Childhood on the Psychological Adjustment of College Females," *Sex Roles* 3 (June 1977): 217-27.

12. Donald C. Doane, *The Needs of Youth, An Evalvation for Curriculum Purposes* (New York: Teachers College, Columbia University, 1942), 1.

Case 2

1. This case was prepared by Stanley Stone and the author.

2. S. K. Saltzman, "Shoplifting: How Much It Can Cost," *Teen* (September 1985): 18.

3. "High Society Shoplifters," *PM Magazine*, WHAS-TV, Louisville, Ky., August 1, 1989.

4. Quoted in "Shoplifting: An Awful Way to Get a Record," *Seventeen*, August 1984, 198.

5. T. B. Maston and W. M. Pinson, *Right and Wrong?* rev. ed. (Nashville: Broadman Press, 1971), 88f.

6. Saltzman, 40.

7. DeMott, "Light Fingers," *Time*, December 31, 1984, 51.

8. "High Society Shoplifters," *PM Magazine*, WHAS-TV, Louisville, Ky., August 1, 1989.

9. Merton P. Strommen, *Profiles of Church Youth* (St. Louis: Concordia Publishing, 1963), 152-55.

10. Merton P. Strommen, *Five Cries of Youth*, rev. ed., (San Francisco: Harper and Row, 1988), 83f.

11. "Con Artists Stealing in the Name of God," *Detroit Free Press*, August 8, 1989, 1a.

12. Art Toalston, Baptist Press in *Florida Baptist Witness*, June 15, 1989, 12.

13. Reported on *CBS News*, March 5, 1989.

14. Milo Brekke, *How Different Are People Who Attend Lutheran Schools?* (St. Louis: Concordia Publishing, 1974), 123f.

15. A 1969 study by Schab revealed that more than 90 percent of high school students have cheated at various times and 97-99 percent said peers had cheated or cheated regularly. Schab's 1979 study revealed that 56 percent of college-bound and 62.9 percent noncollege-bound admitted cheating on tests. Frank Schab, "Honor and

Dishonor in the Secondary Schools of Three Cultures," *Adolescence* 6 (1971): 145-54; "Cheating Among College- and Non-College-Bound Pupils, 1969-1979," Clearing House, 1980, 53, 379-80.
16. Maston and Pinson, 15-20.
17. Ibid., 33-4.
18. Quoted in "Shoplifting: An Awful Way to Get a Record," *Seventeen*, August 1984, 199.

Case 3
1. This case was prepared by Skip Shephan and the author.
2. M. L. Farber, *Theory of Suicide* (New York: Funk & Wagnalls, 1968), 4.
3. Gerald R. Adams, and Thomas Gullatto, *Adolescent Life Experiences* (Belemont, Calif.: Wadsworth, 1983), 474.
4. A. Alvarey, *The Savage God* (New York: Random House, 1972).
5. Adams and Gullatto, 481-88.
6. "Someone Finally Takes a Step Toward Preventing Youth Suicides," *The Courier-Journal*, May 19, 1981.
7. "Squabbling with Siblings Hurts Home Life Most, Surveyed Kids Say," *The Courier-Journal*, March 11, 1987.
8. "Town Where 4 Teens Died in Suicide Pact Tries to Fathom Why," *The Washington Post*, March 13, 1987.
9. "Two More Youths Take Their Own Lives," *Courier-Journal*, March 14, 1987.
10. James Dobson, *Hide or Seek*, rev. ed. (Old Tappan, N.J.: Fleming H. Revell Co., 1979), 173.
11. Bill Blackburn, "Suicide . . . A Cry for Help," *Baptist Standard*, December 7, 1983, 8.

Case 4
1. Quoted by John R. Adams, *The Sting of Death*, leader's ed. (New York: Seabury Press, 1971), 5.
2. Reported in Richard Des Ruisseaux, ed., "People," *The Courier-Journal*, October 20, 1989, section A, 2.
3. Merton Strommen, *Five Cries of Youth*, rev. ed. (San Francisco: Harper and Row, 1988), 99.
4. Adapted notes from a lecture by Wade Rowatt to students in the author's class entitled "Case Studies in Youth Ministry."
5. Earl Grollman, ed., *Explaining Death to Children* (Boston: Beacon Press, 1970), 3-27.
6. Harold S. Kushner, *When Bad Things Happen to Good People* (New York: Schocken Books, 1981), 26*f*.
7. William G. Justice, *When Death Comes* (Nashville: Broadman Press, 1982), 67-85.
8. Richard Ross and Judi Hayes, comps., *Ministry with Youth in Crisis* (Nashville: Convention Press, 1988), 131-34.
9. Ibid., 143*f*.
10. Selected from the forty-three item "Self-Test for Stress Levels" in Keith W. Sehnert, M.D., *Stress/Unstress* (Minneapolis: Augsburg Publishing House, 1981), 68*f*.
11. "Talking to Children About Death," National Institute of Mental Health, 1979, 9.

12. Elisabeth Kubler-Ross, *On Death and Dying* (New York: Macmillan Co., 1969) 34-121.

13. Ruthe Stein, "If You Stand Up Well to Life, You'll Do All Right in Death," *San Francisco Chronicle,* May 25, 1980.

14. Strommen, 99.

Case 5

1. Observations from Sharon Wolfe Sanders, psychiatric social worker, Home of the Innocents, Louisville, Ky., May 1, 1987.

2. Figures reported by the U.S. National Commission on the Year of the Child on April 21, 1980. Any current improvement in these figures is highly unlikely.

3. Quoted from Sharon Wolfe Sanders.

4. Reported in *Florida Baptist Witness,* April 17, 1980, 16.

5. "American Humane Association," *Youthletter,* May 1984, 39.

6. Reported in *The Courier-Journal,* April 15, 1989.

7. Ibid.

8. Mauareen Dowd, "Rape: The Sexual Weapon," *Time*, September 5, 1983, 29.

9. Ann Wolbert Burgess, *The Sexual Victimization of Adolescents* (National Institute of Mental Health, 1985), 48.

10. Jan Lundy, "Ministry in an Abusive Crisis," *Ministry with Youth in Crisis,* ed. Richard Ross and Judi Hayes, (Nashville: Convention Press, 1980), 105-13.

11. Merton P. and A. Irene Strommen, *Five Cries of Parents* (San Francisco: Harper and Row, 1985), 179-84.

12. Murray Straus, "Family Patterns and Child Abuse in Nationally Representative American Sample," *Child Abuse and Neglect* 3, U.S. Government Publication Report printed in March 1979.

Case 6

1. Casewriters are Robert A. and Alice F. Evans, *Casebook for Christian Living* (Atlanta: John Knox Press, 1977), 43-45. Used with permission from authors and Case Study Institute.

2. *London Times*, November 10, 1986.

3. Ibid.

4. ISR Newsletter, Winter 1988, 3.

5. Update on Human Behavior, "I Can Quit Any Time: Alcoholism in America," 7:2, 2.

6. George F. Will, "Koop's Last Crusade," *The Courier-Journal*, July 18, 1989, section A, 5.

7. "Study Contends Alcohol Undertaxed," *The Courier-Journal*, March 17, 1989, section A, 5.

8. "Drop in Arrests Linked to Higher Drinking Age," *The Courier-Journal*, February 1988.

9. Reported on "Action 11 News," WHAS-TV, Louisville, Ky., August 16, 1989.

10. Mike Brown, "Washington Tidbits," *The Courier-Journal*, August 13, 1989, section B, 4; Mike Brown, "Watch Hidden Meaning, Distillers Tell Writers," *The Courier-Journal*, August 13, 1989, section B, 4.

11. Stephen Gibbons Mary Lou Wylie, Lennis Echterling, and Joan French, "Patterns of Alcohol Use Among Rural and Small-Town Adolescents," *Adolescence* 21 (Winter 1986): 887-900.

12. Ibid., 897-98.

Case 7

1. Case is written by Louis Weeks and used with permission from the author and Case Study Institute. See *Casebook for Christian Living* (Atlanta: John Knox Press, 1977), 94-99.

2. Ray Conner, "Drug Abuse: An Epidemic," *Church Recreation Magazine*, July—September 1989, 32-33.

3. "Drug Survey Has Good News and Bad News," *The Courier-Journal*, August 1, 1989, section A, 30.

4. Also see "Drugs: A Deadly Game" developed by the Drug Abuse Task Force S2000, Boy Scouts of America.

5. Reported in "On Target" published by the National Federation of Teachers (NFT), November 1988, 2. NFT grants permission for "On Target" to be quoted.

6. Conner, 33.

7. Adapted from Roger L. Abington, "Helping Teenagers Beat Addiction," *Home Life* 37 (March 1983), 8.

8. Ibid., 9.

Case 8

1. This case was prepared by Philip Hedgecoth and edited by the author.

2. *The Interpreter's Bible* (New York: Abingdon Press, 1953), 10:164.

Case 9

1. Richard Armour, *Through Darkest Adolescence* (New York: McGraw-Hill, 1963), 174.

2. One ten-year-old mother was reported by Barbara York, director of Teenage Parenting Program, Jefferson County Public Schools, Louisville, Ky., in a classroom presentation on March 15, 1989, The Southern Baptist Theological Seminary, Louisville, Ky.

3. "The Facts: Teenage Childbearing, Education, and Employment," Center for Population Options. Washington, D.C., January 1987.

4. "The Facts: Young Men and Teenage Pregnancy," Center for Population Options, Washington, D.C., July 1987.

5. Selected from J. B. Fowler, "Teen-age Pregnancies," *Baptist New Mexican*, April 4, 1987, 2.

6. "Teen Pregnancy: The Facts," Kentucky Department for Health Services, Frankfort, Ky., n. d.

7. "Doubts Voiced that Consent Law Will Cut Number of Teen Abortions," *The Courier-Journal*, April 7, 1989, section A, 1.

8. Information in this paragraph adapted from Lena Williams, "New Codes for Teen-Agers and Sex," *The New York Times* and reported in *The Courier-Journal*, March 5, 1989.

9. Reported on "20/20" TV program, April 7, 1989.

10. "Study Shows Church Kids Not Waiting," *Christianity Today*, December 18, 1988, 54-55.

11. Williams.

12. These suggestions were adapted from certain ideas proposed by Earlene Grise-Owens in a class presentation on March 6, 1987, The Southern Baptist Theological Seminary, Louisville, Ky.

Case 10
1. Case was prepared by Michael Lee Adams and the author
2. Jane Bryant Quinn, "Charities Are Trying to Recapture the Nation's Gift of Giving," *The Courier-Journal*, December 29, 1988, section B, 12.
3. Ibid.
4. Philip Yancey, "Whatever Happened to Charity?" *World Vision* 32 (December 1988-January 1989): 8-9.
5. Orrin Morris, "RD Digest," April 1987, 1.
6. Reported by David Wilkinson, "Signs Indicate Stall in 5-Year Upward Trend in American Charitable Giving,"*Baptist Message*, January 8, 1987, 1.

Case 11
1. This case was prepared by Karla K. Buhl and the author.
2. The following publications produced by the Sunday School Board of the Southern Baptist Convention 127 Ninth Avenue North, Nashville, TN 37234, can provide helpful information: *Church Recreation Magazine, Successes in Southern Baptist Youth Ministry, Summer Youth Ministry Ideas, Youth Ministry Planbook 3 & 4, Bible Studies for Special Occasions*, and *52 Complete Retreat Programs*.
3. Glenn E. Ludwig, *Building an Effective Youth Ministry* (Nashville: Abingdon, 1979), 74-75.
4. A. M. Adams, *Effective Leadership for Today's Churches* (Philadelphia: Westminster, 1978), 96*ff*.
5. G. Douglass Lewis, *Resolving Church Conflicts* (San Francisco: Harper and Row, 1981), 136-40.
6. Adapted from ideas of Jay Hall, *How to Interpret Your Scores from the Conflict Management Survey* (Corne, Tex.: Teleometrics, 1969); Alan Filley, *Interpersonal Conflict Management* (Glenview, Ill.: Scott, Foresman, 1975); and Lewis, 74-92.
7. Louis and Carolyn Weeks, Robert A. and Alice F. Evans, *Casebook for Christian Living* (Atlanta: John Knox Press, 1977), 49.

Case 12
1. This case was prepared by Henry Tyson and the author.
2. Evelyn Felker, *Raising Other Peoplw's Kids* (Grand Rapids: Eerdmans Publishing Co., 1981).
3. Quote in James J. DiGiacomo and Edward Wakin, *Understanding Teenagers: A Guide for Parents* (Allen, Tex.: Argus Communications, 1983), 113.

Part 3
1. LeRoy Ford, *Using the Case Study in Teaching and Training* (Nashville: Broadman Press, 1969).
2. Lawrence Kohlberg, "Stages and Sequence: The Cognitive-Developmental Approach to Socialization," Essays on Moral Development, vol. 2, and *The Psychology of Moral Development*, (San Francisco: Harper and Row, 1984), 49. Also see Robert F. Biehler and Jack Sowman, *Psychology Applied to Teaching*, 5th ed., (Boston: Houghton Mifflin Co., 1986), 76.
3. See examples in Sidney Simon, Leland Howe, and Howard Kirschenbaum, *Values Clarification* (New York: Hart Publishing Co., 1972).
4. Louis and Carolyn Weeks, Robert A. and Alice F. Evans, *Casebook for Christian Living* (Atlanta: John Knox Press, 1977), 72.